"My take-away from the book is that there is good news and bad news. The bad news is that we, as business leaders, can't just sit and wait for luck to come our way. To make the most of our business opportunities takes a combination of luck and hard work. The good news is that after reading *Optimizing Luck,* you'll have what it takes to make the most of that hard work. I look forward to putting these tips into practice for my organization."

—JULIA J. LOUGHRAN, PRESIDENT, THOUGHTLINK, INC.

"Meylan and Teays provide an inspirational lesson on how to establish a culture of working together to optimize luck and mitigate risk. They provide insight into how to adapt these practices to general business cultures to establish more productive and satisfying work environments. *Optimizing Luck* is a must read for anyone trying to establish a successful business culture."

—GENE ALLEN, COAUTHOR, COLLABORATIVE R&D; DIRECTOR OF
COLLABORATIVE DEVELOPMENT, MSC SOFTWARE

"The techniques described by Meylan and Teays work. I had the good fortune to see them in practice firsthand when Meylan was on my team helping to build a consulting practice from initiation to a successful international service."

—FRANK D. VEZZI, OPERATIONS CENTER MANAGER FOR A LARGE
INTERNATIONAL GOVERNMENT SERVICES FIRM

Optimizing Luck

Optimizing
LUCK

What the Passion to Succeed
in Space Can Teach
Business Leaders on Earth

Thomas Meylan and Terry Teays

DAVIES-BLACK PUBLISHING
MOUNTAIN VIEW, CALIFORNIA

Published by Davies-Black Publishing, a division of CPP, Inc., 1055 Joaquin Road, 2nd Floor, Mountain View, CA 94043; 800-624-1765.

Special discounts on bulk quantities of Davies-Black books are available to corporations, professional associations, and other organizations. For details, contact the Director of Marketing and Sales at Davies-Black Publishing: 650-691-9123; fax 650-623-9271.

Davies-Black and its colophon are registered trademarks of CPP, Inc. Evolving**Success** is a registered trademark of Digital Clones, Inc.

Visit the Davies-Black Publishing Web site at www.daviesblack.com.

Printed in the United States of America.
11 10 09 08 07 10 9 8 7 6 5 4 3 2 1

Library of Congress Cataloging-in-Publication Data
Meylan, Thomas
   Optimizing luck : what the passion to succeed in space can teach business leaders on earth / Thomas Meylan and Terry Teays. — 1st ed.
     p. cm.
   Includes index.
   ISBN 978-0-89106-222-6 (hardcover)
   1. Organizational effectiveness. 2. Organizational change. 3. Success in business.
   4. Management. I. Teays, Terry. II. Title.
   HD58.9.M494 2007
   658.4'09—dc22

                                         2007016039

FIRST EDITION
First printing 2007

To Susan-Marie and Carol

CONTENTS

PREFACE

This book captures the leadership methods of a group of people who didn't realize how exceptional they were: the group who ran NASA's first major satellite astronomy observatory. They built the U.S. side of the scientific operations of the International Ultraviolet Explorer, or IUE. Nothing of its kind had ever been attempted before.

One of our colleagues on the project, and still one of our best friends, is Rich Arquilla. Arguably, he's the reason we wrote this book. At his farewell dinner, leaving his Computer Sciences Corporation (CSC) position at the Space Telescope Science Institute, he stated that IUE was "the best damned project I ever worked on." That's no small praise, given that he'd worked on five NASA projects while employed with CSC. But virtually everyone who worked on the IUE project still feels the same way. That makes this a big story.

We contacted and interviewed all the founding managers of the IUE project Science Operations Center, both NASA and CSC management. We learned a lot, especially as common themes began to appear. Many people spoke about simply working hard. Others spoke about keeping their eyes open for opportunity, or planning for problems before they came up. Surprisingly, with only one or two exceptions, people said that they were just lucky.

It turns out that if you listen for it, you will almost always hear the biggest winners in business say the same thing, and they really mean it.

We interviewed Rich Arquilla as a member of the management team in place at the end of the IUE project. He also said something that puts luck in perspective, at least as far as doing business as a manager in that project goes: "Luck is a sort of a spice. If you don't have the main ingredients, then luck won't get you by. It helps everything else to work." If you aren't always in the process of putting together systems to optimize the advantages that come your way, it won't matter whether opportunities knock or not.

In this book, we identify the main ingredients of our project's success and translate them for your use. Most of these are highly relationship dependent; they involve issues like trust and creating real care for customers. The more people in your business who base their habits on these ingredients, the more powerful your corporate culture can become. It acquires focus across your enterprise.

The sources of corporate habits are the leaders and managers. If these habits are practiced in highly visible ways, they can be observed and emulated by workers all down the line. The more they are shared and exercised by everyone in your organization, the more productive your people will be. And, if the history of the International Ultraviolet Explorer project sets a precedent, your people will experience a much greater level of job satisfaction.

ACKNOWLEDGMENTS

We would like to thank the many people who helped us complete *Optimizing Luck*. Our friend and former colleague, Dr. Richard Arquilla, was the first person who urged us to write this book. Throughout the project Rich remained one of our most valuable sources of insight and constructive criticism.

Our research into the origins of the outstanding culture that existed at IUE led us to interview many of the people who started the project. Their historic information, as well as their willingness to spend time discussing their thoughts during those early days, was invaluable to our analysis. The "founding fathers" included Dr. Albert Boggess, Dr. Peter Perry, Dr. Barry Turnrose, Dr. Chi-Chao (Charlie) Wu, and Randy Thompson.

We also talked to several of our contemporaries at IUE to bring out more details and get alternate viewpoints to our own experiences. Our thanks to Rich Arquilla, Thomas Walker, Andy Groebner, Charlie Loomis, Jim Caplinger, Dr. Nancy Oliversen, and Dr. Yoji Kondo.

A number of our colleagues read part, or all, of our manuscript and gave us valuable feedback. We thank them for their generous donation of time, which immensely improved the final product. These reviewers were Dr. Sethanne Howard, Rich Arquilla, Al Boggess, Jim Burke, Donna Weaver, Christiam Camacho, Pat Macomber, Limor Schafman, Dr. Martin Evans, Carol Roxbrough, and David Slifer.

At Davies-Black Publishing, Connie Kallback championed our book from its earliest stages of development and provided us with helpful advice and encouragement. Laura Simonds schooled us in many important issues concerning a genre and marketplace that were new to us. We thank them both.

The analysis and shaping of the key concepts for *Optimizing Luck* took up a lot of our time, as did the actual writing. We spent many weekends and evenings away from our significant others, yet they remained completely supportive and encouraging throughout the project. It is to them that we dedicate this book.

About the Authors

Thomas Meylan, PhD, is a writer and speaker who deals primarily with issues of corporate culture engineering, luck optimization and fault tolerance, and the disciplined use and expansion of collaborative work techniques in organizations and businesses. Based on his career experience, he also works with scientists and engineers to help them successfully transition into management roles.

Meylan served as director of the IUE Data Analysis Center at the International Ultraviolet Explorer astronomy satellite mission during the early 1990s. Subsequently, he provided system integration consulting services to major companies in the Washington-Baltimore region. He currently leads Evolving**Success**® (www.evolvingsuccess.com), a small think tank that studies potential applications of evolutionary psychology to business performance improvement and to dealing with social issues. He holds a PhD degree in astrophysics from Georgia State University.

Terry Teays, PhD, works at Johns Hopkins University, where he is assistant director of the Maryland Space Grant Consortium. He began his research career in astrophysics as first a resident astronomer and then supervisor of telescope operations at the International Ultraviolet Explorer Observatory. Later, he went on to manage a corporate center for scientific research, projects as a government contractor, and his own consulting company.

In recent years Teays has concentrated on managing projects related to science education, including heading the education programs for the Hubble Space Telescope and directing NASA's Origins Education Forum. His current position focuses on developing the future workforce in Maryland for the aerospace community, especially NASA. Teays has received several NASA Group Achievement awards and served on many peer review panels. He holds a PhD degree in physics from the University of Nebraska–Lincoln.

INTRODUCTION

Do some people in business really get all the breaks? Are others continuously blindsided with business disasters? Do some business-people encounter opportunity after opportunity but remain incapable of exploiting them?

That depends on how you look at things.

Differences in levels of success often come down to differences in personal habits. People employ decades-old systems of habits to get through the day. However, most people put no special thought into developing these systems. They pick up a few tricks from mom and dad and a few teachers and a lot more from their peers, while growing up and going through school. And that's where their habit-developing effort stops.

Successful people, in contrast, work hard and continuously on their systems of habits. They know what they want to get out of each day and out of life in general. To get what they want, they study what it takes and learn the skills to obtain it. Furthermore, they often have to train the people around them to focus their energy on what they want to accomplish, too.

The big winners in business, from the execs at Virgin "Everything" and Microsoft to the leaders of highly successful small businesses, prepare themselves and the people around them to handle unpredictable events. They engineer as many elements of their business environment as they can to help them respond effectively to rapidly changing conditions. They observe everything they can, and what they can't observe directly they delegate someone to watch. When these highly successful people land the next big deal or complete the next project ahead of schedule and under budget, they will likely tell you, "Well, we were just lucky."

How do business leaders do this? You might ask, "How can I prepare myself, my team, and my context for an unknown future? Do I have those skills? If I don't, can I get them?"

The key to managing the unknown is found in a cluster of *luck-optimizing* habits we've uncovered among successful people. When unforeseen events give these people an advantage, they capitalize on that advantage. They exploit that bit of luck.

What do these people do when unforeseen things go against them? For bad situations they have another set of habits, which we call *fault-tolerant* habits. Before things go bad they have already put in place resilient safeguards against disaster. Of course, that's not always enough. In addition to these tough-minded business practices, these people have habits that encourage them to engage the problem as if it were an opportunity—because usually it is.

During our research for this book we worked with a lot of people who had practices and habits of luck optimization and fault tolerance. While studying these habits we learned that the best organizations are filled with luck-optimizing and fault-tolerant people and processes. Organizations that don't perform as well seem to be staffed with people, including the leadership and management, who fall apart in bad situations.

Our research also shows that this shouldn't be a surprise. The people who claimed that luck was on their side also had two pieces of advice, usually captured in this single sentence:

"Hire the right people, and let them do their job."

You can't optimize your luck if you don't hire people who can optimize theirs. And if you keep them from doing what they do well, through micromanagement or some other detrimental practice, you will create a fault-*intolerant* system.

We uncovered luck optimization when we researched our professional pasts. We were managers in one of the world's most successful and longest-lasting international satellite astronomy projects (a fairly complicated business!). The management practices at this project were so effective that its planned five-year mission was extended by almost fourteen years. What we learned there about building and leading teams was equally effective when we built and managed groups in other business contexts. If we've done our job right in this book, you can make use of this project's key managerial practices, too.

The International Ultraviolet Explorer (IUE) satellite project is where we met and where we learned how to help people be successful and retain their enthusiasm about their work. It was an international collaboration between NASA, the European Space Agency (ESA), and the British Science Research Council. These government agency partners achieved great success because of excellent satellite design and construction, exemplary engineering operations support, and science operations support. The business of the IUE project was to provide astronomers around the world with a product: scientific research data that, at that time, could be obtained nowhere else.

We are writing about the managerial habits of the Science Operations part of the project. That is where we worked. That is where we learned how to manage and how to lead. That is where we observed the largest concentration of luck-optimizing people in our professional histories. We were working for Computer Sciences Corporation (CSC) at that time, which had the contract to run science operations for NASA.

If we say that this book is about luck optimization, then we also have to talk about how to make it easier to do. IUE managers were adept at handling their business environment. During our research into the project's history, we came to appreciate long-term colleagues as people who naturally practiced luck optimization and fault tolerance. What did they do that you can do, too?

First, when things go your way, be ready to take advantage of the situation, to be opportunistic. Piece together systems of habits that will optimize your chances of success during these conditions of good fortune.

Second, be ready to handle the inevitable times when things don't go well. Disasters happen. People let you down. International agreements fall apart. Governments shut off your funding. Equipment 23,000 miles out in space quits working. You have to have practices already in place that allow you to handle these types of shocks.

IUE managers used these practices to prepare for an unknowable future. We believe they can work in your organization, too.

After this introduction we describe the main principles. Part One, "The Groundwork," Chapters 1 through 4, includes a business-oriented story of the IUE project, the descriptions of both luck-optimizing and fault-tolerant systems and practices, and the type of leadership it takes to make use of these systems and practices.

In Part Two, "The Practices," Chapters 5 through 10, we describe specific competencies that apply to any business or organization, such as hiring good people to create a luck-optimizing team, delegating tasks to these people and letting them do their job, and learning to apply the right amount of human capital to the tasks at hand.

Part Three, "The Culture," Chapters 11 and 12, presents a model that shows the effects of luck-optimizing practices as you manage and lead. It also contains approaches for developing luck-optimizing practices within your workforce to build a luck-optimizing corporate culture.

Luck-optimizing leaders have additional habits that also fall into two broad categories. The first category is defined by being ever alert and observant. All the clues to success and failure are in your business environment and marketplace. Keep your eyes open. The second category is defined by relationship skills. Issues of trust, team dedication, customer focus, and clear communication came up again and again in our research into the project, and in our practices as managers.

When we tried to distill the essence of the project's success down to a single phrase, we came up with the staff's belief in the "sanctity of doing things right." We use the word *sanctity* intentionally, because *doing things right* had that level of importance to the people involved with this project. Doing things right wasn't just a nice goal; it was blasphemous to not do your best. Who is responsible for creating a value like that in a team? Why, you, the leader or manager, of course.

When all is said and done, leaders must build corporate cultures where every member of the organization learns and practices the arts and crafts of luck optimization and fault tolerance. The corporate culture is your top-level luck-optimizing and fault-tolerant system. It incubates the habits of success for all your people. Luck optimization and fault tolerance aren't merely managerial skills. They should be the habits of every person in your organization. This is also the source of energy for continuous market domination by your organization.

We are proud of our place in history. American Science Operations at IUE shut down in 1996, but even as long after shutdown as March 2005, participants at a Washington Academy of Sciences meeting were clearly aware of and impressed with the reputation of IUE. These were government contractors who had made no use of the International Ultraviolet Explorer, but they knew and appreciated IUE's reputation.

We deeply enjoyed the opportunity to serve the scientific public during our tenure with the project, and we are pleased to bring to the business community this guidebook of practices and perspectives based on the history provided to us by every generation of management at the IUE project.

THE GROUNDWORK

PART ONE

The Success of the International Ultraviolet Explorer Project

I find that the harder I work, the more luck I seem to have.

Thomas Jefferson, third u.s. president

We knew from experience that the corporate culture of the International Ultraviolet Explorer (IUE) project was extremely effective, so we set out to understand the origins of that culture. Our research and analysis of the culture's background were aimed at extracting principles useful in improving the effectiveness of other organizations. It was surprising that, for all the complicated factors involved in running a spacecraft mission or a modern business, we could boil all the practices down to the management of changing circumstances, whether good—what we call *luck optimization*—or bad—what we call *fault tolerance.* These two powerful ideas form the foundation for the story that follows.

If you had scoped out the IUE project as a potential investment, you would have seen an exceptional corporate culture driving a powerful business model. The obvious signs of business success would have been apparent: high levels of productivity, product quality, and customer satisfaction. In other words, you would have found the same signs of success that you need in your business.

The project was an outstanding piece of high-tech business. It remains a legend among astronomers (the project's primary customer base). Since you are probably not in the business of operating scientific satellites, the natural question is "Does any of this relate to me and my enterprise?" Yes, it does. After IUE, we managed other government and private sector departments and business units with great success. The methods and procedures we took from the management culture of the IUE project helped us greatly in those later responsibilities.

PROJECT SUCCESS THROUGH CUSTOMER SUCCESS

Let's look at the success of a scientific satellite mission from a business-oriented perspective. The goal of the project was to provide scientific data products to astronomers—the customers, called *guest observers*. The project also supplied supporting services, software products to analyze the data, and expert advice. This business setup facilitated success in two target areas: enabling production efficiency and ensuring customer satisfaction.

Enabling Production Efficiency

In terms of satellite operations, enabling production efficiency meant staging functions on as tight a timeline as possible. Aiming the satellite at a star, exposing its cameras, and reading down the images all took time. The shorter the schedule for this process, the more data a guest observer could collect during a chunk of observing time. After collection, the data had to be processed quickly enough for the observers to plan their work for the next day. Keep in mind that we were running an enterprise-wide pipeline production system to produce individually customized products for each scientist. Efficiency in delivering the product to the customer helped build IUE's great reputation.

Project management also had to make optimal use of limited financial and human resources. Throughout its tenure, the project operated on a cash-poor, understaffed basis. Later space missions of a similar nature took the lessons we learned and established more generous budgets in their start-up proposals. Yet, while those projects may have been better funded, IUE still outperformed them on a dollar-for-data product basis. Running lean worked. (We will build on this fact in Chapter 8.)

Ensuring Customer Satisfaction

The second target was customer satisfaction. Our customers' success as scientists largely defined the project's success. Perhaps you measure success in terms of things like return on investment, donations collected, or market share. Scientific output has equivalent metrics. For example, scientists publish papers and articles that contain new research results in professional journals. The number of scientific publications based on IUE data products exceeded 3,500 at the time the satellite was shut down. This was the largest number for any satellite observatory at that time. In addition, the publication of new findings continued at an impressive level for many years after the shutdown of the satellite, as customers continued to use archived data products for new research projects.

These performance targets were a matter of corporate pride for the IUE staff. Everyone, from the resident astronomer helping the scientist collect observational data to the data tech spinning computer tapes, consciously worked hard to support the success of our guest observers. (We will describe the effect of this collective pride in Chapter 11.)

MARKET DEMAND FOR GREAT PRODUCTS AND SERVICES

More than two thousand astronomers used the International Ultraviolet Explorer Observatory to acquire data products. This was roughly half of the active astronomers around the world. No other observatory on the ground or in orbit has had that kind of market share. In addition, more than five hundred students used IUE data products for their doctoral dissertations. These young scientists also contributed to the steady growth of the IUE customer base.

One key to that level of market acceptance was the openness of IUE to the entire astronomy community. Seniority in the scientific community was not a criterion for access to the satellite. Everyone with a good scientific problem to investigate had an equal chance at using the satellite. Consequently, a lot of young people got their start in space-based science there. As many businesses have learned, catching the young consumer secures a customer for a long time.

But market share without a revenue stream doesn't mean very much in business. Customers have to be willing to pay for your goods or services. Our project was supported by tax dollars. How did it survive? The customer base exclaimed long and loud to the federal government that it was getting great return on its investment in this type of science. The products and services were the best. This was a clear demand that the government continued to satisfy. Happy customers who are noisy customers are a wonderful thing.

Just how did this satisfied customer base affect the project? The mission of the IUE satellite was designed to last three to five years. When the satellite was finally shut down, it had been in operation for almost nineteen years. Customer demand kept the satellite working. Why? Because the customers appreciated the IUE habit of "overdelivery."

OPERATIONAL EFFICIENCY

Efficiency was a key target in the IUE project's corporate culture. The efficiency with which the project collected and generated data products was noteworthy, especially when compared with other unmanned NASA science missions. What is most impressive is that this efficiency level remained constant throughout the project's lifetime, even in the face of ongoing degradation or outright failure of components on the satellite as it aged. IUE project management invested time and resources to preserve the level of productivity expected by the customers. Project workers updated software, enhanced operational procedures, and improved the scheduling process to maintain customary levels of performance for the scientific community.

As we studied the ways IUE personnel kept productivity up, we discovered the use of two closely related types of systems. By *system* we mean something more than "computer system." *System* here means a collection of methods and procedures, some of which might be computerized, but many of which might not. We call one class of these systems *luck-optimizing systems,* which are used to capture or create advantages (or profits) when conditions in the business environment go your way. (These systems are described in Chapter 2.)

We call the other class *fault-tolerant systems,* which ought to accomplish three things for you and your organization. First, they should reduce the impact of any misfortune your organization experiences. Second, they should facilitate rapid recovery from a major disaster. Third, as do luck-optimizing systems, they should generate advantages (or profit) for you in spite of adverse conditions. (You can read about these in Chapter 3.)

But back to efficiency and productivity. To begin, you can't know what your efficiency is if you aren't measuring the right quantities in your business process. The project had defined and tracked a good number of simple and easily understood quantities from the beginning of the mission in 1978. The majority of these merely measured various aspects of productivity: how many images were processed this week, or how long it took to do a special, one-off task. Most of these metrics were required by the contract with the government, as part of the project's accountability to NASA. The staff, however, was also interested in monitoring its performance by the same metrics.

For instance, during the eighth year of operation (1985), a key component of the satellite failed. Because of that failure we needed to invent a new way to aim the satellite. The project had planned for this possibility and had replacement procedures ready to run when it happened. We knew exactly how hard this event hit the mission, as illustrated in Figure 1. We also knew exactly when previous efficiency levels had been restored.

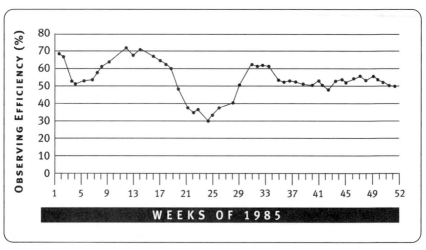

FIGURE 1 ► IUE OPERATIONAL EFFICIENCY

CREATING PRODUCTS
THAT RETAIN THEIR VALUE

People still buy a lot of recordings of the Beatles' music. The books by Mark Twain still sell well today. And scientists still download a lot of IUE data products, even though new ones haven't been made in more than ten years.

The original guest observers had a one-year period during which they had exclusive rights to the data collected for them. After that, the data products went into a public archive, available for anyone to use in scientific research.

The first IUE project scientist, Dr. Albert Boggess, wanted a data archive to be an important feature of the project. Boggess wanted a true *people's satellite.* He believed that standardized, accessible, and easy-to-use data products would create demand. This was a real innovation and cultural change in the space science community. In business terms, Boggess was broadening his customer base. He actively encouraged all scientists to use the archive, and he made sure its products were easy to use.

Many businesspeople take this shared usability for granted today. However, at that time, every computer brand had its own operating system. Every computer application had a unique file format that no other application could use. Making data products universally accessible was a major technical challenge.

The IUE archive was not just a collection of data products. It was also the anchor point for an array of customer services. It included an extensive suite of research-grade software products. Project staff trained researchers in the use of this suite of software tools. So, in addition to generating a highly sought-after product, the project also provided first-rate support services and technical help for end users.

It wasn't long into the mission before as many data products were being downloaded from the archive by scientists doing research as were being added to the archive by new observations. And that downloading rate increased every year. In one five-year period (1987–1992), the use of archived data products increased approximately 400 percent. Keep in mind that a customer downloading a data product is equivalent to a sale. If you achieved 400 percent growth during a five-year business expansion plan, you would be quite pleased.

Today, more than ten years after the satellite was shut down, the archived data are still being used for research and new scientific results continue to be published. What's the lesson here? Delivering good product generates significant traffic and keeps the product relevant for decades.

EVOLVING WITH TECHNOLOGY

The IUE project led the way in using new technology to enhance its services. Many of its innovations are now industry standards. IUE customers continually adopted new technologies as they emerged. The project revamped many customer-facing business processes accordingly. For example, we began using the World Wide Web, a few years after it became available, to deliver IUE data to both guest observers and archival researchers. (Other examples of IUE innovation are discussed in Chapter 7.)

In 1992 we used new technology to upgrade the control center hardware and software. We knew we could simultaneously expand customer services and reduce operating costs by doing so. Among many new capabilities, the system allowed guest observers to conduct their observations from anywhere in the world, using Internet-based capabilities. Before, they had to go to NASA's Goddard Space Flight Center in Greenbelt, Maryland, to personally direct activities during their observing time with the satellite.

New technology also affected the product line. Originally, film negatives of the images were provided to the customer, as well as computer-generated paper plots of the data. These were very expensive. As the customer base took up desktop computing for research work, the project began to deliver computer files only, and eventually discontinued its hard-copy product lines. This saved production costs while providing the same level of service.

The project constantly improved its data products as well. IUE employees continually studied the quality of the data the satellite produced. They understood how camera age affected image quality and how satellite temperature altered the characteristics of an image. Their growing knowledge always went back into improving the products.

In addition, new methods for squeezing every drop of information out of the satellite's data products were always coming online. Techniques came from both customers and project staff. New techniques were validated by the staff before incorporation into the IUE archive's suite of software tools.

There also were two formally organized feedback groups of customers in advisory roles. This partnership with the customer base eventually led to a new, archive-standardizing data processing system. The entire archive of IUE data was reprocessed, using this system, to produce a uniform and improved set of data products.

INNOVATION IN CUSTOMER ORIENTATION

IUE was successful in another way. It developed a new model of how to run a NASA spacecraft mission. As noted, it was Al Boggess's vision that IUE data products would be accessible to any customer with a good research idea. Nationally funded observatories on the ground traditionally operated this way, but satellite observatories up to that point had been operated as projects limited to a group of team members with exclusive ownership of the data products.

Boggess's vision for the IUE mission meant that all the observing time on the satellite was up for grabs. Competing proposals were judged each year by panels of astronomers to determine the best scientific use of the satellite. Anyone could apply. There was no restriction by institution, college degree, or employment status; even staff members of the project could apply for satellite time. The influence of the International Ultraviolet Explorer on the astronomy community was, and continues to be, substantial. The project introduced many astronomers to satellite astronomy and created an ever-growing demand for its data products.This type of operation has been used by many of the most successful astronomy satellites that followed IUE, such as the Hubble Space Telescope, the Spitzer Space Telescope, and the Chandra X-Ray Observatory. The IUE project had developed and refined an exportable business model.

Because the customers were used to a particular type of service at ground observatories, IUE processes were developed to provide a similar experience. This allowed guest observers to adapt quickly to IUE's service, which reduced their ramp-up time and helped capture them as regular customers. They became both experts on space-based astronomy and ready customers for NASA's subsequent spacecraft missions.

The project also provided training for future NASA satellite astronomy operations. Computer Science Corporation's (CSC) success at NASA Goddard made it the natural choice to handle other science missions based there. CSC moved IUE employees to several other NASA missions, including the Hubble Space Telescope and the Far Ultraviolet Spectroscopic Explorer, and used their expertise to exploit these new opportunities.

The IUE project was a great success in terms of sustained growth, market penetration, customer satisfaction, and production efficiency. And, the staff thought it was a great place to work! Much of this success was due to its business culture. Was IUE lucky? Sure, but its culture optimized its luck.

And that is exactly what this book is about.

LUCK-OPTIMIZING SYSTEMS

Luck still plays a part in success or failure, but luck favors the competent, hardworking manager.

JERRY MADDEN, NASA (RETIRED)

Luck optimization is the skill of squeezing every success-creating advantage out of any situation. A luck-optimizing system is a set of methods and procedures *you* create to amplify your natural abilities to succeed in any environment or changing set of conditions.

Luck optimization is a skill managers must practice. It is a skill you seek and nurture throughout your organization. Luck optimization must make its way into your people's attitudes and skill sets and your documented methods and procedures. In the end, luck optimization has its most concrete expression in the luck-optimizing habits practiced by every person in your organization.

THE CORNERSTONE OF
A POWERFUL CORPORATE CULTURE

As we've transplanted methods from the International Ultraviolet Explorer project into other business settings, we've typically improved team productivity by a factor of two to three. On a few exceptional occasions we've hit a factor of ten. We attribute these results to the luck-optimizing practices we learned at IUE. We used them in new contexts and those around us began to use them. As a result, we saw increased creativity, innovation, and productivity.

Al Boggess, the man at NASA who got the IUE project rolling during the early 1970s, started out with a team that always searched for ideas, techniques, tools, or whatever they needed to do the job better and improve service to the customers. That searching evolved into what we now identify as luck optimization, and it remained alive in the project through to the end. This chapter uses parts of that history to illustrate how luck optimization can operate in a business context full of challenges and risks.

A LITTLE HISTORY ON LUCK OPTIMIZATION

In the early 1970s, Al Boggess spotted a gap in coverage—a time when the country would not have a major astronomy mission in orbit. A string of missions was about to end, and the mission that eventually became known as the Hubble Space Telescope wouldn't go up until 1990. The European Space Agency (ESA) was in a similar spot and was actively seeking an advanced astronomy project to put into orbit. If ever there was a moment to design and pitch to NASA a major new mission, that was it.

Boggess's timing was right, but merely filling a gap wasn't his only motive for a new mission. He also wanted to do something that hadn't been done before. He wanted to put a telescope in orbit around Earth and make it available to anyone who had a competitive scientific proposal. This concept was an innovation. Previously, astronomy satellites had been developed with the leadership of a senior scientist from academia, who pitched the project to NASA for fabrication and launch. The scientist would then have something of a proprietary lock on the scientific results and would control who got access to the satellite.

The opening hurdle for Boggess was selling his approach to NASA and the then-current leaders in space-based astronomy. Fortunately, Boggess had two strengths on his side. First, he had good rapport with the leaders in this scientific community. After he sold them on the concept, he optimized his luck by coaching them to make supporting pitches to NASA leadership. Second, although Boggess did not know NASA leadership well enough to close the deal, his immediate supervisor, Les Meredith, did—and Meredith was willing to go to bat for the concept. With the supporting pitches made by key astronomers, Meredith secured the go-ahead from NASA headquarters for what became the International Ultraviolet Explorer project, with Boggess as its first project scientist.

Then it came time to pull the scientific team together. There weren't many people with expertise in running satellite-based astronomy missions in those days, but Boggess got lucky again. Two reputable astronomers, Charlie Wu and Al Holm, became available at just the time he wanted to form his team. Wu and Holm came on board as contract scientists to work on IUE operations. Both were highly respected for their accomplishments on a series of satellite missions called the Orbiting Astronomical Observatories. They had the most extensive hands-on satellite operations experience for space-based astronomy that Boggess could possibly get.

"They understood the project," said Boggess. "One of the great pieces of luck we had at IUE was that we were starting to put together an operational staff just as the funding for the project that they had been on was closing out." Now, this reference to luck might be just a casual phrase. However, many people associated with the IUE mission spoke of luck coming at critical times.

We asked Charlie Wu about these early times in the mission. "For us, it was the opportunity of a lifetime," he said. Basically, Boggess outlined what he wanted the mission to be like, and then he left it to the contractors, as full peers in the mission, to accomplish it. Even though it was hard work, things went well from a variety of viewpoints. "Everything . . . all the planets seemed to line up from the very beginning," said Wu.

LUCK-OPTIMIZING LESSON

How did Boggess get the IUE project going? The answers are important to any project's success.

• He kept his eyes open and spotted an opportunity: a gap in NASA's astronomy missions.

• He had key relationships that could make things work the way he wanted. If he didn't have direct access to a potential stakeholder, he knew someone who did.

• He had luck in timing: The best people possible for the job were just becoming available. They were the best technically for the project, and they had the hardworking temperament he wanted as well. What else was there to do? Boggess hired them and let them do their job.

PROFILE OF LUCK-OPTIMIZING LEADERS

Boggess and Wu weren't the only managers from the start of the IUE project to make serious reference to luck. More to the point, they weren't the last managers in the project to take advantage of luck, either. By the time we came on board, taking advantage of favorable conditions was a strongly entrenched habit. Based on our interviews with the founding fathers of the project, we concluded that the corporate habit of taking advantage of good fortune started at the very beginning.

IUE management had a habit of succeeding in most of the circumstances surrounding the project. What habitualized abilities let them take advantage of fortunate circumstances? Why did these habits seem so pervasive at all levels of the project? How did they persist for the nearly two decades of the project?

Reflecting on our experience in the IUE culture and combining our thoughts with the living history from those who started the project, we've isolated five characteristics that lead to the ability to create luck-optimizing systems. Luck-optimizing leaders

- *Foster connections to the world.* They have an extensive network that connects them to the important people in their external business environment (market leaders, policymakers, customers, suppliers, other large-scale influencers).

- *Observe continuously.* They are always aware of the conditions in their business environment.

- *Work hard.* They not only are hardworking, but, because they are exceptionally observant, they identify the right things on which to expend their efforts.

- *Think critically.* They identify and work on the right things because they carefully test the information they gather from their business environment, assessing it for clues leading to success.

- *Stay in it together with the working teams.* They have an effective network of relationships with the various working groups that actually perform the services and create the products that generate the revenue and keep the customers (in-house and external) happy.

When we compare the habits that were in place at IUE while we worked there with the habits of those who started the project, we find a lot of similarities. The profile of luck-optimizing leaders was the same for all phases of the project. The leadership habitually formed and nurtured relationships with the influencers (Congress, NASA, and scientists) who could dictate whether the project lived or died. They kept an eye on everything from policy shifts to talent availability to the health of the satellite. They worked hard. They critically assessed what they observed to make the best use of the time and talents of those working for them. And, they stayed close to their working teams.

IUE managers were connected to their customers, their sources, and their workers. Why is this important? These relationships helped them establish priorities and showed them where to focus their skills in observation and critical thinking (that is, testing the information coming from their business context) to get the most out of their hard work.

Without a good connection to their customer base or their work teams, all their clever insight into their market and all their hard work would have been a waste of time. Business is about connecting with a need in the marketplace, having the human capital to produce a solution to that need, and getting the solution to market. Without relationships there is no foundation for a luck-optimizing system.

The five characteristics of luck-optimizing leaders supply the core of habits for the entire corporate culture. Let's look at them in detail.

Foster Connections to the World

This concept is best illustrated by the examples of leaders who have created luck-optimizing systems. Al Boggess at NASA had the solid technical skills and the connections with the scientific community to get his concept off the ground. He needed the political savvy of Les Meredith to sell the project to NASA HQ, and they collaborated to make it happen. After the project was approved, NASA involvement was actually quite light. At the time, CSC held a general science support contract at NASA Goddard, which allowed Boggess to bring Wu, Holm, Skip Schiffer (another astronomer), and other science support personnel on board as contractors.

The chain of command leading from that CSC contract at Goddard to the top of CSC was populated by people who believed in NASA for strictly idealistic reasons. Involvement with NASA was a matter of pride for then CEO Bill Hoover, and he supported it wholeheartedly. This created flexibility in the business relationship that remained mutually beneficial to NASA and CSC throughout the life of the project. While this greatly facilitated the achievement of Boggess's goals, it also created favorable conditions for CSC to expand into a wide range of space science support opportunities later on.

Peter Perry was one of the first scientists hired by CSC to work on the IUE project. Perry was soon assigned as CSC's task leader for the project, and over time he built and ran CSC's Science Programs business unit. He explained that, back in the mid-1970s, NASA was building on a string of highly visible successes that began with the Apollo moon landing program. And furthermore, at that time NASA provided the brightest point of national pride in the post-Vietnam, post-Watergate era.

While connections to the money, via NASA, and the intellectual horsepower, via CSC, were vital to getting the project going, the key connections were to the potential users: the international community of scientists. Boggess invited a number of them to serve on the IUE Users Committee before launch to help design the mission and the hardware to go into orbit. A satisfied scientific community reciprocated by urging NASA to keep IUE going when budget crunches threatened its existence. These connections built a strong and enduring IUE mission.

To sum up the importance of relationships in the wider world: Al Boggess had key connections. He worked them until he got momentum on his side to get the IUE project started. In the NASA scheme of things he was something of a junior-middle manager at the time. His relationships made up for any lack of status that otherwise might have held him back.

Observe Continuously

Human beings have senses for a reason. We use them to figure out what's going on around us, and then we respond accordingly. This is a simple truth, yet mind-numbing routines often keep us from looking up every once in a while to check on the world around us.

Building new luck-optimizing habits is completely dependent on the observational powers the business leader brings to a situation. Here's one example. When we asked Charlie Wu how various tasks fell to people, including leadership roles, he gave us a good look into the early days of the project.

> At that time, we sort of looked at what people were good at, and essentially let them do that. . . . Now, of course, when we were there the organization was not very big, but we kept our eyes open to see who had the leadership potential: how they got along with people, and whether or not they could read people. And when we saw a person

LUCK-OPTIMIZING
LESSON

If you are in a situation where you want to make things happen, consider your network and ask these questions:

- Do you know everyone you need to know?
- If not, who do you know who can help you make things happen?
- Do you have a good concept and a good story to tell about it? A good story can make the people you need want to be involved and, then, you've optimized your chances for success.

who was leadership material, we'd make him a task leader in charge of some small area and let him grow from there. So, it was all from observation—what we thought and what we saw, what people's potential was.

The main purpose and benefit of observing employees, according to Perry, is, "If you put a person into a place where he is useful and feels useful and feels successful, everybody's happy."

People are the most significant feature of a business environment, and Wu's use of observation to assign tasks and assess leadership skills speaks volumes. This approach to talent management entails a high level of interaction. Absentee managers aren't going to be able to accomplish what Wu and other IUE managers did simply because they won't have the data on people to make the right decisions.

Work Hard

Peter Perry hired Barry Turnrose, before the launch of the IUE satellite, to work on various aspects of image and data processing. Everyone in the project was working hard prior to launch, but after launch it became clear that the effort it would take to run operations according to project requirements had been badly underestimated. The project had committed to twenty-four-hour turnaround time in processing the data so astronomers could plan their next day's observations (in case something unexpected happened). What hadn't been anticipated was the condition of the raw satellite data. They tended to be in pretty bad shape and required a lot of special work just to get them to a point at which they could be processed into good scientific data products. Turnrose related the following story.

> We were running twelve-hour shifts, and Peter and I were working an alternating schedule. After a while, both of us, I remember vividly, were walking down the hall at shift change like twins, rubbing our stiff necks because we both had some kind of a virus. . . . I don't know what to say about how we did it. I think probably everybody . . . felt that failure was not an option. You know . . . it's an easy phrase to throw out, but I think that everyone really did have the feeling that this just had to succeed. Once you've gone all through that you have a "band of brothers" sort of feeling.

This seemed to create a sense of ownership that pervaded the entire project. Both Perry and Turnrose commented on the feeling of family within the project that seems to persist to the present, even though the project was shut down in 1996. Our experience is that this feeling ran all the way down to the workers we managed.

Wu relates similar conditions in the operation of the satellite. He, Holm, and Schiffer ran the satellite on an 18/7/365 basis for the first three years of the mission. (Europe handled the other six hours of the day.) That was it . . . three people on an 18/7 schedule. Wu said,

> We jumped in and were all trying to do a good job. . . . Since there were only three of us we didn't want to be a burden on either of the others. So when one got sick we still dragged into work because if we stayed home one of the other two had to come in on their day off, and that was an imposition that we didn't want to put on the other guy.

This work ethic also created managerial advantages in the area of leading by example, according to Wu.

The new people that we hired, the telescope operators, see that Skip
and Al and I work so hard and never complain and just try to do the
work. That essentially rubs off on people. When they come in, that's
the only way to work. . . . The whole atmosphere rubs off on the other
employees. If people come into an organization and people start bick-
ering, backstabbing, then that's the organization that you're going to
get for the long term. But if you trust everyone to come in, and everyone works and tries to do the best job that they can, that's the atmosphere that gets passed on.

Like family cultures, corporate cultures get passed down by employees emulating leaders. A hardworking culture requires hardworking
leadership.

And hardworking teams are usually better at producing systems that
optimize their chances for success. After all, if they're going to work
hard, they're going to want a lot of return on the effort they are investing. A good system makes the most of the output of those efforts.

Think Critically

Working hard is vastly better than hardly working, but working hard is
not enough to optimize a venture's chances for success. You have to work
smart, too. As IUE project scientist Yoji Kondo said, "Business is always
an empirical process. You're always testing against results." This idea of
testing both what you observe and what you do is the core of critical
thinking. Testing in the business context can be as simple as asking, "Did
this process get us what we wanted?" or as complex as asking, "What are
the adjustable components in this process, and how does making adjustments in one place alter the rest of the system?"

Earlier in the chapter, we referred to the use of observation in sorting out technical talent and leadership skills. It took a rigorous standard
to make use of those observations. Most IUE managers used themselves
as a standard of performance: "I want a hardworking person, like me."
"I want a person I can trust, like me." "I want a person who can sit down
and solve tough problems, like me." IUE managers watched for familiar

skills. They knew what they were looking for, and it went well beyond mere technical capability.

That said, you might argue, "Everyone picks people like themselves. What made you IUE guys different?" The difference is that we weren't looking for everybody's personal process and style to be like ours. We wanted new hires to achieve results with the same quality, in the same volume, and in the same time frame as we did . . . or to do even better. How they got their results was only important if we could learn something new from them to improve our processes. That's how we applied critical thinking in hiring.

Critical thinking, as a component of a luck-optimizing system, is always about testing for best possible results. IUE leadership used critical thinking to handle human capital issues like hiring. They also had to use critical thinking to form the technical solutions that got the satellite running at its best. The need for critical thinking never stopped. Everyone had to think sharp to keep the satellite running well, especially after components on it started failing.

In the early 1990s, for example, it was necessary to revamp the ground control system that ran the satellite and obtained the scientific data requested by the guest observers. It had been in place since before launch in 1978, and, between the wear and tear on the hardware on the ground and the failure of hardware on the satellite, a new ground control system was needed to sustain the necessary level of productivity. The computers that controlled the science operations had begun to fail regularly. On some shifts the main computer and both backups failed. Once, a component in the control room caught fire during operations. Teays used these incidents in presentations to NASA, CSC, and the Users' Committee to gain approval for spending the funds to upgrade the system.

With approval in hand, Teays had to get started on integrating a completely new network of computers and adapting the old software to them. Fortunately, he didn't have to bring in a crew of system integrators to build this system. That saved the project a lot of money. He was "lucky" in being able to pull together a project team largely drawn from the people already working on IUE. This luck derived from IUE's

LUCK-OPTIMIZING LESSON

Critical thinking is what you use to evaluate a system at all stages of its development, rollout, and operation. Answer these questions about your system:

- Will (or does) the system optimize your group's chances for success?

- Does it exceed expectations?

- If it doesn't, does the system still produce a useful enough effect that it should be continued?

- Have your success targets changed?

- Do you now need something that works better? Or differently?

ability to hire the best people and to give them opportunities to continually expand their skills on the job.

Much of Teays' staff's time away from telescope operations was spent in tasks that sharpened their computer expertise. For several years people in his shop were asked, "What would we need to replicate current operational functionality and add capabilities to streamline as many IUE processes as possible?" In response, various team members focused on different technical aspects of the project. Some concentrated on the computer replacements; others worked out software to replicate current capabilities; yet others worked on new functionality to make life easier in operations and to speed things along to other parts of the project. In effect, building this new system was merely an extension of tasks they were already handling. This cultural habit optimized the chances of success in reinventing the ground control system.

In addition, Teays made meaningful use of his CSC connections to deal with network security issues: The new system to operate the spacecraft needed to be secure against computer hacking. It also needed to be able to deliver new data directly and safely to the image processing system. Ron Pitts, the senior scientist heading this project, had formulated a security solution, but this wasn't his area of expertise. Teays contacted another division of CSC, which provided network support for a major federal security agency, and asked them to review Pitts's security design for potential problems. Again, it was plain good luck that CSC had some of the best security people available, and Teays took advantage of it. These experts gave the plan a clean bill of health, and this assurance of security became part of the presentation that obtained approval from Goddard's network security board to build the new system.

Stay in It Together with the Working Teams

A key component of IUE's leadership style was close interaction between managers and workers. The traditional CSC management structure worked well. The presence of line managers facilitated the kind of inter-action required to keep project tasks focused and moving forward as required. But, it wasn't merely the structure that worked. Without managers who were interested in the tasks they managed, the IUE mission would only have been a short-lived backwater project attached to the mainstream of NASA's science activities.

The majority of the project's line managers were selected from its line workers. Few workers actually sought management responsibilities. They saw the "real work" as too much fun and management as too much responsibility. So, as they had done from the beginning, upper IUE management usually picked the new manager who demonstrated the best skills with people.

In most cases, the managers remained contributing members of the team at some level, meaning, yes, they still got to do some of the fun work. It also kept the team cohesive, as the managers remained close to the teams they managed.

The teams appreciated that a change in management status didn't create class distinctions. If the manager guided, that was OK. If the manager had to lead by direct example, that was OK, too. Working hard together built esprit de corps in the IUE project. Because of this, teams within the project rewarded their managers with dedication to the project's needs.

REQUIREMENTS OF
LUCK-OPTIMIZING SYSTEMS

We've spent a lot of time describing the characteristics of people who construct and work in luck-optimizing systems. We used the history of the IUE project to illustrate how they operated—with heavy emphasis on relationships, being observant, thinking critically, and just plain working hard.

Why spend so much time on the characteristics of luck-optimizing managers instead of on the systems themselves? This is because luck-optimizing systems develop out of the mind-set of determination to use current conditions as a springboard for success. A luck-optimizing manager encounters a new problem and asks if an old solution will work or if a new one is needed.

Luck-optimizing systems tend to be situational, but the principles used to build them aren't. That's why we emphasize the characteristics of luck-optimizing people over the nature of the systems.

That said, are there any general features that you might expect to see in a luck-optimizing system?

Keep in mind that when we talk about a luck-optimizing system, we are talking about a collection of personal habits that the manager uses or a collection of corporate habits that everyone in the company uses. These habits may be standardized methods and procedures, or they may be broad guidelines for approaching any changing situation. Let's identify some basic requirements for luck-optimizing systems.

- The system should be as simple as possible.

- The system should be self-improving and/or self-correcting.

- The system should guide users' attention onto the process they are working.

- The system should supply guidance and help in unclear situations.

- The system should generate confidence in users that they can successfully complete the process.

- The system should clearly identify those who should be participating in the process.

This set of system requirements is used to build luck-optimizing systems where any combination of people, automation, and computerization is involved to carry out some business process or function. Let's take a look at each requirement.

The System Should Be as Simple as Possible

Simplicity tends to optimize your chances of success. Complexity reduces them. Obviously, the more complicated an approach to a problem, the more that can go wrong. Complex systems are also harder for people to use, even if they get the special training needed to use the systems successfully. No doubt there are times when a business process needs to be driven by a complicated system. However, whenever possible, stick with the simplest possible solutions to get your products and services to the market.

The System Should Be Self-improving and/or Self-correcting

Some methods and procedures may allow you to run blindly along even though things are going desperately wrong. You don't want those in your business or organization. You want methods and procedures that pop up good and useful warning flags whenever people working a process need them to keep on a good track.

Part of what makes a system self-improving or self-correcting is the level of attention you pay to it—in other words, how you observe and critically evaluate the results you're getting from the system. For instance, do people frequently complain about the difficulty of making a system work? Do the same complaints or errors crop up again and again? Why do they? The system is telling you, "I need to be improved or corrected." Listen to it, and start working on the improvements or corrections as soon as you understand how the system creates its own problems.

The System Should Guide Users' Attention onto the Process They Are Working

Have you ever worked with a software program to do something, but you couldn't figure out where to start? Did a process have so many capabilities that you didn't know how to find the one you wanted to use? Or have you ever had a system do things "for you" that you simply didn't want done and you couldn't turn off?

A luck-optimizing system helps users focus on what needs to be done. For example, such a system might start by asking, "What would you like to do?" and then suggest several possible ways to get started on that task. Further, once you get going, the system should not be so full of bells and whistles that your attention is diverted from the task.

The System Should Supply Guidance and Help in Unclear Situations

Perhaps you can recall a time when a software tool you were using left you stuck in a task and couldn't guide you out of a difficult part of a process. Does the same hold true for the management and leadership functions in your business processes? When people need guidance is it available? Even a well-thought-out set of methods and procedures can leave a worker lost. When that happens, where does guidance and help come from? Are your technical experts, subject matter experts, and last, *you*, arrayed in such a way that the gears of your business processes don't jam up when someone has a question? A luck-optimizing system gets information to the people who need it in the shortest time possible to ensure that the process keeps moving toward profitability and customer satisfaction.

The System Should Generate Confidence in Users
That They Can Successfully Complete the Process

How many of your employees are afraid of screwing up with a computer? How many are afraid of screwing up *any* of your business processes? That fear is not helping your business succeed. And if your systems are bad enough to inspire anxiety in your workforce, you have systems that are strongly luck eradicating.

People ought to be able to understand and do anything they've been assigned to do and trust that the tools you provide will get them to a successful finish. People at the IUE project were really smart, and the last thing they wanted to do was waste time trying to understand something that was supposed to make them productive in five minutes or less. We often had the wherewithal to rebuild what we needed. Your people may not have the necessary skills to do that, so make sure the systems you give them to help them do their job actually help them do their job.

The System Should Clearly Identify Those
Who Should Be Participating in the Process

There are times when the system is composed entirely of people. Because we ran pretty lean at the IUE project, we couldn't afford to move people around unnecessarily or make assignments without careful thought and planning. For example, we wouldn't put the project's least socialized techie on a sales call team where millions of dollars were at stake. Likewise, you wouldn't send an obviously unqualified person on a technical call to solve a major customer's problems. When you design a system to implement a business process, the necessary human skill sets must be included in the plan, and, if possible, the system should sit idle until the appropriate human skills are in place and ready to function.

OPPORTUNISM

Good bridge players are dealt, on average, the same quality of hands as everyone else, yet they consistently come out as winners. Granted, they have more skills, but they also take every opportunity, no matter how small, to increase their chances of success. They even give their opponents opportunities to make mistakes.

Allow us to clarify something about the preceding sections. You might think that we just defined the characteristics and components of a luck-optimizing system. Well, yes, we did. But, more to the point, this set of characteristics allows you to build operational luck-optimizing systems that reach into every corner of your business activities. What we just described is the core of a corporate culture that optimizes the chances of success for everyone involved in your venture.

When we talk about optimizing a venture's chances of success, we're talking about people making habitual use of a highly opportunistic worldview. Not merely *optimistic*, but *opportunistic*. This is an aggressive psychology from a market-conquest point of view.

One might say, "Well, opportunists are bad because they exploit people and situations." There certainly are opportunists who take unfair advantage. But we're not talking about illegal or unethical behavior. We're talking about a quality in professional people that allows them to find legitimate business advantage in every circumstance and in everything they attempt to do. They always look for ways to tip the odds in their favor.

Consider the following example. Toward the end of the IUE mission, NASA authorized the reprocessing of the entire archive of IUE data (at that time, twelve years' worth) with a new, standardized version of image processing software. The big hurdle was to make sure the software could run on two completely different types of computers, one in Europe and the other in the United States, and come up with the same results. We got the needed solution in place in both locations.

As it turned out, the computers dedicated to the reprocessing and re-archiving did not provide enough computing power to complete the task in the time NASA and ESA wanted it done. A new generation of computers was starting to be used in other parts of the IUE project; but, of course, these were completely different from the two types already in use. The project decided to use the new computers anyway during off-peak hours to make up the deficit.

Various teams wrangled for about two weeks trying to figure out how to use these totally different machines. Eventually Meylan was asked to help puzzle things out. After the teams described the problem, he asked, "What makes this problem any different from the one we already solved in making the U.S. and European systems compatible? Nothing you've told me indicates that we can't use our current compatibility strategy with these new computers." Was Meylan such a genius? No. Everyone at the meeting knew the answer. They were just distracted by the challenges of the moment. We all know how bringing in fresh eyes can sometimes make a big difference in finding needed solutions. Getting the fresh eyes there in time is a corporate-level luck-optimizing habit. In this case, that one simple observation saved perhaps a thousand hours of labor on a problem that had already been solved.

That's opportunism.

View the characteristics of luck-optimizing leaders and systems as the foundation of your business behavior habits. The more that people base their habits on those characteristics, the more powerful and focused your corporate culture can become.

The sources of these corporate habits are the leaders and managers. If these habits are practiced in highly visible ways, they can be observed and emulated by all workers down the line. The more these habits are practiced by all the people in your organization, the more productive everyone will be.

And if the International Ultraviolet Explorer project sets a valid example, your people will also experience a greater level of job satisfaction.

LUCK-OPTIMIZING
LESSON

The clues, tools, and resources for success are usually available in your immediate surroundings. For clues, tools, and resources that are a little further afield, draw on your network. If you have good supporters and suppliers, they understand that your success enhances their success. Even with their assistance, it's important to keep your eyes and ears open to catch vital information about your business situation. You still must cover the essentials:

- Work hard to make things happen.

- Judge, weigh, test, and assess both your information flow and your work output to ensure that you are getting where you need to go.

Fault-Tolerant Systems

*It is impossible to make anything foolproof
because fools are so ingenious.*
Murphy's Law, section 11

It's good to be poised to take advantage of opportunities, but it's not enough. Opportunities aren't all that fortune throws at you. On the International Ultraviolet Explorer project, we had to develop principles for fighting unforeseen misfortune, as well as known risks. Both opportunity and misfortune are real-world elements of your business context, and you want to have systems of habits in place that help you optimize the return on your preparation for both types of situations.

WHEN LUCK GOES BAD

We use the term *luck-optimizing systems* as a shorthand way of describing methods and procedures that optimize your chances of success under changing conditions. For the management of misfortune or risk, we turn to computer technology for the term *fault-tolerant systems*. The main idea is this: A fault-tolerant system remains productive regardless of what goes into it or what happens around it. For instance, you might want a business software system that figures out what you want it to do, or at least doesn't damage any data assets, even though you give it completely ridiculous inputs. Or you might have a computer system that still works accurately (though perhaps a bit slowly), even though half of it was destroyed by fire and fire-fighting sprinklers.

You want your entire corporate culture, and all of its systems, methods, and procedures, to be fault tolerant—that is, to continue working effectively regardless of the changes your organization experiences. The less impact bad luck has on your organization, the more fault tolerant it is.

Here's a quick review of the system elements of the IUE corporate culture described in Chapter 2:

- Leaders and managers have an effective network of relationships that connects them to the important people in their external business environment: market leaders, policymakers, suppliers, other large-scale influencers.

- Leaders and managers are observant, continuously aware of the conditions in their business environment.

- Leaders and managers are hardworking. Because they are also observant, they tend to be working hard on the right things.

- Leaders and managers work on the right things because they carefully test the observations they gather from their business environment, assessing them for clues leading to success. This is the habit of critical thinking.

- Leaders and managers have an effective network of relationships with the various working groups that actually perform the services and create the products that generate the revenue and keep the customers happy.

These elements work well for taking advantage of opportunities. Now consider some misfortunes that could occur with no warning:

- A vital relationship changes or ends through death, conflict, or a change of one party's priorities.

- A vital resource suddenly, and maybe permanently, becomes unavailable.

- A superior competing product or service appears in the market.

- A critical piece of equipment fails.

- External circumstances drive a radical change in the schedule.

- A key employee or leader leaves the organization.

- Your key market moves out from under you.

- A basic element of infrastructure collapses as a result of storm damage, fire, or any other cause.

Could a fault-tolerant corporate culture effectively weather these unanticipated problems? That's just what such a culture is designed to do.

A SIMPLE STARTING POINT

In the early 1980s the IUE project established an innovative service: a pair of facilities designed to help astronomers use the data collected from the IUE satellite. One, in Colorado, was closed in 1992. Meylan took over management of the other, at Goddard, in 1993 and renamed it the IUE Data Analysis Center (IUE DAC, or simply "the DAC"). As he got to know the staff he also began learning more about fault-tolerant systems than he had thought possible.

Up to that point, most astronomers wrote their own software to conduct their research. Although their programs might be used to calculate extremely complicated scientific models, they were relatively simple. Each program usually had only one feature: Use a certain data set, run it through a certain process, and spit out the answer. Any desired options usually were included at the beginning of the input data.

In contrast, the DAC had to provide versatile software that could satisfy the wide range of scientific work of IUE's customers. The software had to be user-friendly, with lots of features, and it had to be robust. It had to be able to withstand whatever any user might try to do with it and deliver whatever results the user needed. The DAC accomplished this by developing a standardized format, naming conventions, and hooks between the various programs so that all the procedures worked together.

There was at that same time a bright, dedicated IUE staff astronomer who had a talent for inadvertently crashing software systems. We'll call him Nelson. Like most astronomers, Nelson was quite good at computer programming, and that was a large part of his duties. Sometimes his job was to break software. When he intentionally set out to break a program he was fairly successful at it. But when he wasn't trying to break software, he was fabulous at it.

So, the programming staff at the DAC developed a simple hierarchy for grading the resilience of the software it produced. Here are their certification levels, in reverse order, for defining the fault tolerance of their software products.

3. Foolproof fault tolerance

2. Astronomer-proof fault tolerance

1. Nelson-proof fault tolerance

If Nelson could use your software without a glitch, you had really engineered something special.

This story illustrates perhaps the most common cause of system failure: user error. This isn't limited to computer systems. If your business systems, methods, and procedures are complex, then they will need self-protecting features built into them to tolerate users' mistakes. Good systems help people perform accurately and efficiently each time they carry out a task. They do this either by being simple or by providing enough guidance at each step of the process to ensure successful use.

FAULT TOLERANCE AT IUE

How did the staff at the DAC build fault tolerance into their software? They started by doing two exercises. The first was to imagine as wildly as possible all the things that could go wrong with the software. That, of course, got them a long way. The second exercise was to imagine as wildly as possible all the ways a customer might use their product. That got them a long way, too.

Now, these may seem like simple-minded approaches, but this team had been building experience in this kind of software engineering for nearly ten years. They already had a great collection of software development gotchas on file. Over the years, these gotchas had developed into high-level approaches to the creation of new software products—a never-ending activity at the DAC.

Teays had a different set of requirements for fault tolerance. His team was responsible for collecting data for scientists using the IUE satellite. Minor mistakes could cost the customer valuable satellite time. Further, if an operator asked the satellite to do the wrong thing or point in the wrong direction, it could spell the end of the mission. If a major component of the satellite quit working, it could cause drastic, uncontrollable spacecraft behaviors. How do you plan for these possibilities?

Take pointing the satellite at the correct location in space. Pointing it at the sun would always be bad (way too bright). Pointing it at Earth, or even the moon, would be bad (also too bright). Pointing the telescope at Earth also meant the antennae on the backside of the satellite were directed away from Earth, which impaired the transmission of signals to and from Earth. Also, the solar panels needed to be pointed as directly as possible at the sun to maintain electrical power. How does a fault-tolerant system work to fulfill these requirements?

To build fault tolerance into Teays's team, the telescope operators (TOs) and resident astronomers (RAs) underwent three months of extensive formal training. It involved lots of hands-on experience operating the satellite, supervised by an experienced TO or RA, as appropriate. For their first solo shifts, TOs were paired with an experienced RA; for their first solos, RAs were paired with an experienced TO.

The satellite operations software included both redundancies and safeguards. It usually provided more than one path to obtaining a particular observation, so the operator could optimize the efficient use of an astronomer's allotted observation time. The safeguards served to prevent mistaken commands being sent to the satellite. Many times the software would flash a caution that a particular command would have

LUCK-OPTIMIZING LESSON

The first step in creating a fault-tolerant team is to hire the right people. Screen potential hires for the qualities the project needs. We screened for people who found challenges invigorating rather than daunting. The telescope operators were dedicated to finding ways to provide the best service to the customers, including squeezing the most data collection time out of every shift.

certain consequences. Some options were not allowed, but sometimes you could override the warning if you had sufficient reason.

As new versions of the software were developed, they were extensively tested by the people who would be using them to ensure the highest level of fault tolerance. Testing included following all decision paths, as well as intentional efforts to break the software.

During satellite operations the team always had more than one science operations person monitoring activities. In addition to the TO, the RA oversaw the shift. All activities were also monitored by another team, in the engineering control center, who oversaw the health and safety of the satellite. Having more than one person keeping track of what was happening was cost-effective, especially considering the possible consequences of a major error or missed problem.

The high caliber of staff hired for the operator position, coupled with their level of dedication, solved another problem frequently encountered in production: inattention during routine tasks. Though many of the shifts were apparently routine, the operators always looked for ways to increase efficiency. To them, it was like solving puzzles, trying to make each shift as productive as possible. These self-assigned challenges kept them sharp while on task. On low-activity shifts when it was safe to do so, they could also work on their own research projects or program new software.

THE NEXT THING TO GO WRONG

The orbit of the IUE satellite carried it daily through a part of Earth's magnetic field that collected a lot of electrons. As the satellite plowed through this region, the electrons affected IUE's cameras and degraded the images being taken. When this was happening, camera exposure times had to be kept short to get useful images.

The satellite had a sensor that indicated how dense the electrons were and how badly they would degrade the image. This electron cloud was a major factor in planning the activities for each shift. One of the senior astronomers, Rich Arquilla, was interested in learning more about the effects of the electrons' density and the timing of IUE's travel through them.

Teays gave Arquilla time to investigate this in detail. Arquilla's original motivation for this research was scientific curiosity and an interest in learning new skills, but it clearly related to the project's business environment. Arquilla analyzed the historical record of all the measurements the satellite's sensor had made. His results were published in the scientific literature, which added to the prestige of the IUE project and CSC. It also provided CSC with a more skilled employee.

Continuing his research, Arquilla discovered that he could use measurements from another satellite to predict the time of IUE's passage through the electron cloud and the intensity of the cloud on any given day. His comparison with the results from the IUE onboard particle sensor showed that his predictions were accurate enough for operational use, if needed.

As it happened, a short time after Arquilla finished his work, the onboard particle sensor failed. Loss of this component could have been serious because the scientists would have been taking images without knowing the correct exposure times. This would have resulted in many wasted images and degraded the quality of IUE's product. It could have seriously called into question the desirability of continued funding for the mission.

Using the system Arquilla had developed, we could use the data from the other satellite to predict the time and intensity of the problem. It wasn't as good as the continuous information stream from the particle sensor on the IUE satellite, but it was good enough to plan the shift's activities and produce usable images.

Did Teays know that the particle sensor was about to die? Of course not. If you know things with certainty, you don't have to optimize your luck and develop fault tolerance. It's the things you can't know about the future that should motivate you as a leader to operate in a luck-optimizing and fault-tolerant mode.

APPLICATION IN ANOTHER TECHNOLOGY-BASED BUSINESS

Meylan used similar management methods to develop fault-tolerant systems for other industries after leaving the space program. His first work was in developing a comprehensive customer support system for a company starting up an Internet business. He and his customer worked out projection models for technical support calls, billing support calls, staffing levels and timelines, costs per call, costs of customer support per month per customer, and so forth. They also projected the range of calls they were likely to get and then planned to hire accordingly.

One feature of this system was a knowledge base for problem resolution. This gave an operator immediate access to information about previous solutions to a particular problem. This feature offered consistent solutions and made up for knowledge limitations a particular operator might have, thus shortening the time it took to deliver a solution to a customer with a technical difficulty.

FROM TECHNOLOGY FAULT TOLERANCE TO ORGANIZATIONAL FAULT TOLERANCE

When machines break down or computers crash, the occurrence is, at the least, a great inconvenience. If the breakdown occurs in a mission-critical system at the wrong time, it can be a disaster.

In one sense, the people aspects of a fault-tolerant system are the more difficult ones. People tend to shy away from thinking about potential disasters. This is good if it encourages natural optimism about the future, but bad if it discourages people from thinking about and creating preventive measures and backstops.

Remember, Wu, Holm, and Schiffer were the only RAs able to run the satellite on the American side of the project. They divided two work shifts among them every day for the first three years of operation. In terms of a fault-tolerant system, that stinks. If they got sick they came in anyway because there was no backup with their special skills. Running lean is one thing, but those guys were running all the time. The project survived in spite of inadequate staff size, but it was clearly always at risk. As the project matured, IUE leadership realized that they needed to hire additional staff to improve the fault tolerance of the system.

That's another practical application of fault tolerance: the elimination of *single-point failures*. Here's the basic concept: If you have a business system that requires the presence of a specific person with specific skills, or requires that a single, perhaps one-of-a-kind, piece of equipment always runs exactly as it should, you have a system with a single-point failure. If that one specific person doesn't make it to work, your whole system shuts down. If that one machine breaks down, you're out of business until you get it fixed.

Some single-point failures are easy to fix. For a system that requires a specific person with specific skills, you can train additional people in the needed skills, perhaps in a cross-training program. If the system is dependent on a single piece of equipment, you can order duplicates or change the system to use more common equipment.

At IUE single-point failures were avoided if at all possible. Most personnel were trained in multiple jobs. The different jobs were closely related and had some overlap, but, nonetheless, critical skills were replicated within the staff. Another backup was an annotated call list: If something prevented a person from making it in to work, managers could call in the most appropriate replacement. If necessary, most of the frontline managers could step in and do the work.

LUCK-OPTIMIZING
LESSON

What consitutes a system breakdown for an organization?

- Loss of leadership?
- Loss of faith in the company by employees? Or customers? Or both?
- Loss of the one person who actually understood the filing system?

The simple call list includes an "escalation path." Problems requiring increasing levels of expertise or authority are bubbled up to the appropriate levels in the staff or management network. This strategy keeps a severe problem from languishing because a worker can't solve it or might unintentionally take an inappropriate action. It also keeps a severe problem from getting lost. A problem that gets lost doesn't get solved, and that only leads to graver consequences. A clearly defined escalation procedure for handling problems, or opportunities, is essential.

Now, using call lists and escalation paths may seem like a no-brainer. However, experience tells us that these ideas are by no means obvious to all people in all places. And we know that these practices are not followed everywhere to reduce single-point failures and improve fault tolerance. While one of us was working at a government agency, it had several single-point failures, no call list to bring in other personnel in case of problems, and an insufficient escalation path to keep critical problems in the view of and under the action of appropriate staff or management. Problems at this agency created a breakdown in accountability between employees and their respective companies under contract. Absenteeism was a serious problem. System development and integration were falling behind on a major nationwide installation because no one knew the actual state of the development activities.

TWO SIDES OF THE SAME COIN

The most successful people find advantages in both good circumstances (luck optimization) and bad circumstances (fault tolerance). Advantages can be found—in fact, must be found—in any context. That's your job as a luck-optimizing leader. Collins and Porras in *Built to Last* offer a number of examples of visionary corporations that suffered serious setbacks and turned them into opportunities—and they also offer counterexamples of less successful organizations that didn't.

As discussed in Chapter 2, finding advantages requires constant observation, coupled with an accurate means of interpreting what you observe. Accurate interpretation is an exercise in critical thinking.

IUE project scientist Yoji Kondo described a fault-tolerant organization. Organizations require a certain looseness or flexibility. There are always going to be mistakes and misunderstandings. The organization has to give managers flexibility to deal with issues as they present themselves. If the policy book provides some good advice for what's happening right now, well, then fine. But if it doesn't, the manager has to have the latitude to set aside policy and make new decisions about the issues, including the corrective steps to take.

Though we are talking about fault-tolerant systems in this chapter, don't forget that what's good for fault-tolerant organizations is also good for opportunistic organizations. You can find shelves full of books that include stories of businesses sitting on potential cash cows that they didn't exploit. Why? "Well, because we're not in 'that' business" the head person might say. In seeking opportunity, you also have to have the latitude to set aside long-standing decisions and practices when needed.

A FIRE HOSE RATHER THAN A BOTTLENECK

The IUE project collaborated with another group based at Goddard. This group operated the repository of IUE data, both raw image data and processed data products. It was also the designated supplier of archived IUE data to the public. Its people were pretty slow at getting data properly archived and at getting data out to requesters. The big bottleneck most often was the group's inability to generate computer tapes with the requested data in a timely manner. The project took the public relations hits for this lack of service, and, of course, we weren't happy about that.

Meylan had a good relationship with one of the NASA people involved in that other organization. This individual was interested in new technologies and at that time (late 1992) was getting excited about the World Wide Web. After Meylan started managing the DAC, he and this NASA individual designed a Web-automated system that would allow users to look at the entire IUE data log, select what they wanted, and have it either sent via e-mail or staged to a NASA computer disk from which they could retrieve it. IUE customers were pleased because now they could obtain data at will. The NASA contact was happy because his bottleneck was resolved and the solution also benefitted IUE. The workers responsible for making IUE data tapes were happy because they didn't have to make the tapes anymore. IUE project management, both NASA and CSC, was pleased because the international ultraviolet astronomy community (their customer) was happy.

When we eliminated the need to generate and disseminate computer tapes, we eliminated a single-point failure that had been a continuous point of contention for the project. As a result, scientific research based on archived IUE data exploded and remained huge through the early years of the new millennium. The technology of the World Wide Web allowed us to replace one weak, highly fault-intolerant system with an extremely robust, highly fault-tolerant system. Our fault-tolerant system gave us much more power to serve our customers.

EXCESSIVE EMPHASIS ON THE BOTTOM LINE

Is it fault tolerance or just a fault? Many organizations limit the evaluation of their business processes by focusing exclusively on the bottom line. What kind of fault tolerance can a corporate culture provide when the only feedback a manager gets is "you didn't make your numbers"?

LUCK-OPTIMIZING
LESSON

The best fault-tolerant systems do more than reduce the impact of a problem or speed up recovery from a bad incident. They also help turn adverse situations into opportunities.

The principles for building a luck-optimizing corporate culture and for building a fault-tolerant corporate culture are the same. In your company, you might approach these two ideas explicitly and separately, thereby creating two distinct but related sets of habits. You'll end up with a corporate culture that responds equally well to either opportunity or misfortune. With this kind of culture, any change will be good for business. That's opportunism in a nutshell.

While it's important to monitor the bottom line, it is not enough. Fault-tolerant preparation must be implemented at the operational stage, not the reporting stage. When the quarterly balance sheet shows disaster has already happened, you have waited too long.

Focusing on the numbers of financial performance is not a luck-optimizing practice, nor is it conducive to building a fault-tolerant organization. This limited focus creates a delusion of awareness, promotes laziness, impedes critical thinking, and enables the existence of fault intolerance.

The Delusion of Awareness

First and foremost, a focus limited to financial results creates a delusion that management is looking at all it needs to look at. This is clearly not the case. Observation of an organization's entire business context includes examining:

- Major market trends
- Local market trends
- Trends and changes in the directives of the chief executive levels
- Effectiveness, productivity, efficiency, and ease of use of current business methods and procedures
- Current effectiveness in obtaining and retaining talent
- Current information on customer satisfaction

This wide-angle observation has to be an ongoing, habitual activity. Without this observational activity, there really isn't much of an explanatory connection between financial results and the business processes that produced them. They are simply numbers floating in a business information vacuum.

Laziness

Using just financial results permits laziness among upper management and promotes noninvolvement with the people producing the revenue. This runs completely counter to the IUE project experience, where the managers worked hard and remained closely involved with the revenue-generating employees.

Uncritical Thinking

Using financial results as the chief definition of corporate success reduces the use of critical thinking in the organization. "Numbers don't lie," it is often said. Yes, but by themselves they don't say enough either. They don't tell you how to optimize your chances for success or raise the level of fault tolerance in your organization. You can only get that information by continuously examining your entire business context.

Fault Intolerance

The use of financial results alone creates an inflexible, fault-intolerant culture. People and departments who don't make their numbers are simply eliminated in many cases. From a somewhat Darwinian stand-point this could work as a way of winnowing out weak performers and retaining top talent. However, it doesn't do much to actually prepare workers to solve real problems when they appear. And according to the optimistic Mr. Murphy, they will appear.

An undue focus on the numbers provides virtually no direction for fixing anything. The danger is that if the numbers look good, you just coast, and if they look bad, you slam on the brakes.

LEADERSHIP

It's terribly important for everyone to get involved.
Our best ideas come from clerks and stock boys.

SAM WALTON, FOUNDER, WAL-MART

Leaders don't become successful by being right all the time. Nobody can do that. Effective leaders optimize their luck by systematically trying new things and keeping what works. One of the biggest-payoff skills we transferred from the International Ultraviolet Explorer project to business consulting was experimentation; it works just as well in leadership and management as it does in science.

Where does a leader or manager find the ideas to run experiments that improve business? As Sam Walton points out, one source leaders and managers can tap is their employees. IUE managers did exactly that. This suggests, of course, that there needs to be an ongoing, collaborative relationship between leaders, managers, and employees. Luck optimization and fault tolerance, and the experiments you run to uncover and build these for your business, are strongest when all your people are free, willing, and able to contribute to them.

While many business writers treat leaders and managers as separate groups (because it simplifies the research), for us, a luck-optimizing manager must be a leader as well. This is especially important at front-line and middle management levels. In the collaborative work environment that produces the maximum output from your team, you may designate any team member temporarily to be a leader for a particular project or function. By distributing the leadership among your employees, you maximize the possibility of someone contributing a visionary idea to your business.

We're going to look at leadership based on three themes that emerged repeatedly in our interviews with IUE managers, both government and contractor. Many of the points these managers brought up about leadership, just as was the case with luck, require an interpretive framework. For this we will make use of Evolving**Success** research in applying evolutionary psychology to business environments.

The first theme deals with IUE managers' beliefs about natural-born talent. About half the people we interviewed made statements about management genes or asserted that few people have the innate talent for management or leadership. They said if the innate talent isn't there, it can't be developed with any amount of training.

The second theme deals with business environment (big-picture) issues. Peter Perry, the CSC director in charge of IUE, spoke at length in our interview about issues ranging from the interests of the whole country at a given place and time to the task of getting the right person into the right position and about how this whole spectrum affects the strength of your business.

The third theme deals with leadership and corporate culture. A number of IUE managers commented on how the person at the top strongly influences the culture practiced by those working for that person, using terms like *leading by example*. Of course, the person at the top always is leading by example.

Why did we order these three sections this way? Well, first, we want to discuss the idea of a leadership gene, and if it exists, how it would operate. Second, we've emphasized throughout the book the importance of observation as a luck-optimizing and fault-tolerant skill, so we're providing a thumbnail sketch of the impact of the external business environment on your business. Keeping a watchful eye on the business environment is essential to your success. Third, once you know what you're up against, you can formulate a team and create a culture to build luck-optimizing and fault-tolerant systems—and use them to execute your strategy.

INNATE LEADERSHIP

Over the past thirty years, we have read dozens of books that assert with apparently reckless abandon that everyone can be a leader. We fail to understand why, of all human activities, leadership is often written about as if no required predispositions, or preferential aptitudes, or intellectual skills differentiate potential leaders from those who won't be able to lead. There is perhaps nothing more difficult to perform than leadership, yet writers continue to claim that anyone can do it if they learn the right skills.

Of course, the same assertions can be made about anyone becoming a professional basketball player, an astronaut, or an internationally famous novelist. Such assertions prove nothing about a given person's potential effectiveness in any of these roles, any more than they do about effectiveness in leadership.

Leadership and Management Genes

So does that mean leadership is genetic? Of course not. Most people, we're quite sure, understand the term *leadership gene,* or *management gene,* to be a metaphor. But the metaphor represents something observable to IUE managers, some of them now with thirty years of management experience. They believe strongly in naturally endowed aptitudes and talents for leadership and management that are *not* evenly distributed across all people. Here are some of the things they've said.

> You cannot make a manager out of somebody who never had that [something] to begin with. . . . A guy who doesn't have the concept of treating people fairly, and doesn't show any leadership potential, you . . . just can't make a manager out of that. That instinct has to exist in that

person to begin with. And you see that by the things people do. You . . . don't have to ask them, "Do you have leadership potential?" —CHARLIE WU

I loved teaching. I enjoyed facilitating the Front Line Leadership sessions because it was teaching. And the one thing that I learned from that is that no matter what they say, you cannot teach someone to be a manager. . . . The people that I had then would do so well in the class, but they were horrible managers. . . . They could do whatever they were told in those little practice sessions. But the point is that dealing with people, it has to be something that you just feel is in your system. . . . If you're not comfortable dealing with other people, don't be a manager. Do something else. —PETER PERRY

If the management gene is not there to start with, then there is no chance of success. —YOJI KONDO

To some these might sound like pessimistic statements. But they are not. They are statements made by people who proactively and extensivly sought managerial talent. IUE managers were extremely good at hiring exceptional people, and even among those exceptional hires, only a small percentage were capable of managing or leading.

IUE managers said little more about how they identified potential managers than that they used a combination of observation and gut reaction. That's not quite instructive enough. Somehow, they found new managers who could optimize their luck and generate fault tolerance in their operations. We found good managers during and after our IUE days. What did we find?

Drive-Satisfaction Strategies, Behaviors in Groups, and Leadership

Not only is there the IUE example, but we have examples in our later experience with leadership and management to consider as well. In our Evolving**Success**® work we've identified three primary drives at work in human beings: the drive to avoid or eliminate discomfort, the drive to have sex, and the drive to raise offspring to self-sufficiency in the shortest time possible. The more closely an individual's behavior conforms to these drives, the more successful the individual is as an animal in nature.

Animals and people make use of drive-satisfaction strategies (DSSs) to be successful. Two of these strategies involve competition. The aggressive competitive DSS is called *alpha climbing,* where individuals fight for dominance. The defensive competitive DSS is called *status quo preserving,* where individuals attempt to hang on to status or possessions they have acquired.

Humans mostly live and work in groups. Life in these groups, while highly competitive, provides drive-satisfaction opportunities that could take advantage of collaboration.

Individuals use the collaborative DSS of *leading* if they believe they can get better payoff for their drive-satisfaction activities by coordinating the efforts of a group to help. There is typically little collective strength under the rule of an alpha climber, but a leader can guide a group to generate much greater value through coordinated strength and the optimal use of specialized behaviors.

If someone is using a collaborative leading DSS in a group, others may seek opportunities to cooperate with this leader. The collaborative DSS for these people is *contributing.* Using this strategy, people achieve better payoff for their drive-satisfaction efforts when they lend their strengths and talents to the program run by the leader. Under an alpha climber, all these people can do is hope to guard what they have or find in order to keep it for themselves. Under a leader, they can contribute their time, skills, or resources and expect some kind of added return on that investment in the leader's agenda.

Let's look at some differences between alpha climbers and leaders.

- Alpha climbers view members of the group as competitors. Leaders view members of the group as potential teammates.

- Alpha climbers view drive-satisfying resources (food, water, building materials, tools, and so on) as the prize for attaining the top position in the group. Leaders view drive-satisfying resources as things that can grow if they are handled correctly: with the right solutions, what the group has can be made into something greater.

- Alpha climbers are in it for themselves, period. Leaders are in it for themselves, too, but they understand how sharing the rewards of team success perpetuates group cohesiveness and strength among all members.

- Alpha climbers control everything possible to create the greatest personal advantage in any situation. Leaders get every team member to contribute to the cause with the greatest strengths he or she can muster. Alpha climbers gain advantage by beating every individual in the group. Leaders gain personal advantage by building increasingly successful teams.

Were the managers at IUE thinking about drive-satisfaction strategies, alphas, and leaders as they were looking for new managers and leaders for the project? No, they weren't. But, in practice, they sought out people who approached a group of employees as a team, not as a new roster of opponents.

LEADERSHIP AND OBSERVING THE BIG PICTURE

Big-picture observation is vital to your success. You can't prepare luck-optimizing and fault-tolerant systems to suit current and changing conditions if you don't keep your eyes open to them. This key leadership function of observation separates the winners from the losers.

Twenty years ago, who would have known that today . . .

- Millions of people would feel a need for and have a cell phone

- People would be able to carry their entire music collection with them in their pocket or purse

- A globe-spanning Internet would be vital to business and communication

- The United States would be unable to produce enough skilled knowledge workers to supply the needs of the country's business

- India and China would become the chief sources of knowledge workers for U.S. business, through phones and the Internet

LUCK-OPTIMIZING LESSON

Not surprisingly, you may have observed some people behaving both as alpha climbers and as leaders. Everyone switches DSSs as conditions and abilities dictate. As an example, think about what happens when your nice, collaborative team has to compete against another team. In this case, if you are the leader in the group, you'd better come out swinging like a top flight alpha climber on your team's behalf if your team is going to win.

These changes have changed what's possible in business.

For instance, the argument could be made that the IUE project couldn't succeed today. In the 1970s, when IUE was getting started, NASA and space exploration were still a big part of U.S. thinking. Today, the Cold War is over, so the patriotic fervor that fed our side of the space race is gone. From a business standpoint, it's no longer sexy to be involved with NASA. The public still supports space exploration and is interested in science discoveries such as those from the Hubble Space Telescope, but spending money on space does not have the same urgency behind it.

For the bulk of U.S. business, the twentieth century in America was all about the love of accomplishing big things—until the 1980s anyway. That has been replaced with the love of making money, plain and simple. This shift alone changes the kinds of product and service ideas you can bring to market.

Peter Perry cites this example.

What's valued is how much money we can make. The automobile industry is a good example of that. You know, they put a lot of chrome and plastic and all that on and the car looks nice. I bought a crawler tractor for my forestry work. It's Chinese. Why is it Chinese? You see, the Americans don't make 'em like that anymore. They're all shiny and nice and then they break down. The Chinese are using the same plans that John Deere used back in the fifties, and it works.

Perry also provides this telling example about a major misread of a business context by NASA officials who failed to see the big picture.

[I] was talking to one of the NASA guys, and he said, "You know, we were all so stupid when the space race was going on, and NASA was in the forefront. They were saying that we should do all of this stuff to beat the Russians, because . . . the bigger rocket we build, [the harder for the Russians to compete]. And we all sat around and said, 'If we could just get rid of this war attitude . . . and just do science, we could do so much better.'" Well, when the Soviet Union imploded, all the money stopped right away. And he said, "We should have realized that the only reason . . . the government was giving us all this money for science was because we were building a bigger rocket that we could stick a bigger nuke on top of."

At the time, NASA officials didn't optimize their luck on the basis of this geopolitical reality. If they had used Cold War fears in the public the way the Department of Homeland Security does today, they might have had the largest single federal agency in operation.

Presently, people are more afraid of a terrorist attack than a nuclear attack. That has opened up a lot of new business opportunities, and a lot of companies have scurried to contract with the Department of Homeland Security to provide a wide range of services. Some of these same contractors used to do business with NASA, but they shifted their markets in response to changes in the business environment. They observed and adapted to the changes, and they led their companies into new areas of business.

Perry also suggests another important venue for big-picture observation: your own company. If you haven't observed the priorities of your organization, you can't optimize your luck with respect to the organization's agenda. Perry cites the backing of CSC CEO Bill Hoover, group

president Al Nashman, and division president Arturo Silvestrini as making the Science Programs business unit possible. From the mid-1970s through the 1990s, these three executives were big supporters of NASA for personal and patriotic reasons. The entire executive chain at CSC explicitly and frequently made things happen to ensure that CSC would always be in the business of supporting NASA science. "On the CSC side you had a management structure . . . saying, 'We believe in this. This is a good thing to do,'" Perry said.

You can never collect perfectly complete and perfectly accurate data about your business context, and, fortunately, you don't need to. All you need is enough information to tip the odds in your favor. And it's not like you will stop collecting data at some point; once formed, your habits of observation keep you focused on the big picture all the time.

LEADERSHIP AND CORPORATE CULTURE

Here's the cold hard fact about leadership: If you've been in charge for any length of time, your organization is going to look, and act, and smell like you do.

It's a monkey-see, monkey-do world out there, so leading by example is always the default mode of culture formation. People will rise to your level, or they will stoop to your level.

Does this mean everybody is going to act exactly like you? Of course not. It means that your team's behavior will show the imprint of your behavior—partly because you hired people like yourself, and partly because your team is emulating your behavior.

Unfortunately, the less ethical and the less ambitious you are, the easier it is for your team to emulate your behavior. People naturally exert as little effort as possible to achieve drive satisfaction. They conserve their energy. So even if you lead your team to follow and act on high ideals, they will need frequent encouragement.

Choices in Forming a Culture

Corporate cultures are inherently competitive because human beings are inherently competitive. However, as we discussed earlier in this chapter, people have the capability to collaborate when the opportunity arises and when doing so makes drive-satisfaction efforts easier or more effective. Collaboration is a solution-based approach to satisfying personal drives.

CSC Science Programs (where the IUE project lived within the CSC structure) was a pocket of collaborative culture that thrived within CSC's larger competitive corporate culture. The IUE team was composed largely of scientists, who typically brought a solution-based approach to their work on the project. This solution-based approach lent itself to finding collaborative strategies to apply to the project's operations and problems.

The CSC leaders at IUE had to know how to lead collaboratively within the project's culture and how to compete within the larger CSC culture for general corporate support, bid and proposal funding, and approval for special activities, such as putting a CSC astronaut in the space shuttle. IUE leaders learned how to step out of their scientific, collaborative culture and scrap a bit in the competitive business culture of the CSC hierarchy. They had to do both, so they learned to do both.

LUCK-OPTIMIZING LESSON

The luck-optimizing habits for competitive and collaborative behavior are a basic experimental process applied to your improvement as a leader or manager. If you are not used to being observant, get used to it. If you aren't a great record keeper, become one or hire someone to keep track of things for you. And if you like to watch and keep records better than you like to execute, get your butt out there and execute until it hurts.

How would you train yourself to recognize which combination of competitive behavior and collaborative behavior to use to optimize your luck? Here are some suggestions:

- Observe the market for competitive conditions and collaborative opportunities.

- Observe your team to sort out the competitors, the collaborators, and those who can be both.

- Observe how your team members go about things and identify key behaviors to try yourself.

- Execute behaviors you identify as having potential for improving your personal approach (or more complex methods and procedures, as needed).

- Keep track of the results you get, in terms of

  - Correctly sorting out competitive from collaborative contexts

  - Applying the appropriate behavior to the context more often than not

  - Executing the appropriate behavior effectively enough to improve your luck-optimizing habits . . . and quantifying the improvement and comparing it with previous results

Leadership Beyond Competition and Collaboration

Sorting out the differences between competition and collaboration and understanding how these work in both your market and your organization help you optimize your luck and set up fault-tolerant positions on current business issues. Your corporate culture needs to amplify your competitive capabilities in the marketplace. This will require a mix of competing and collaborating behavior within the organization. You will need to experiment continuously to get this mix right and thus optimize your chances of success.

Keep in mind that your organization will look and act like you if it doesn't already. How do you want your company to look and act? Do you look and act that way?

If there is to be change, *you* will have to change first.

This is where we differentiate ourselves from other management consultants. Many of them will tell you that there are certain practices that all businesses in all places and at all times should be executing consistently. That means all of their clients will end up operating in more or less the same way, with no means of generating business distinctiveness.

In contrast, we're telling you to find your own way in a more or less scientific manner. Try things, keep track of how they worked, refine your approach, and try again. Why? Because by nature we all approach life and business with subtle differences, both advantageous and not. When you operate with the aim of optimizing your luck, you operate to build your strengths into methods and procedures. When you operate with the aim of creating fault-tolerant systems, you operate to minimize the impact of your weaknesses.

You want all your employees doing that, too.

LUCK-OPTIMIZING LESSON

As your organization's leader, you are in charge of determining what characteristics you want to see in your corporate culture. This is where you define your differentiators relative to both your market and the labor pool from which you will hire. What do you want those differentiators to be? Do you want

- A hardworking company?
- A smart-working company?
- A creative company?
- A customer-pleasing company?

The list is potentially endless. Just write out, "What do I want my company to be like?" List the possibilities, and then start working on the new behaviors to make the change.

THE PRACTICES

PART TWO

HIRING

You're only as good as the people you hire.
RAY KROC, FOUNDER, MCDONALD'S

It is interesting that while we worked at the International Ultraviolet Explorer project, we just assumed that the good hiring practices we saw were the normal way of doing business. When we went on to manage in other types of businesses, we learned how rarely good hiring practices are followed.

Every manager we interviewed who was in some way responsible during the start-up of the project said, almost word for word, the same thing about hiring: "Hire the right people and let them do their job." This indicated that the hiring practices at the beginning of the IUE project squared with our practices at the middle and end of the mission. All of the work that went into careful hiring produced a team dedicated to doing things right. This level of commitment must be initiated through the hiring process. That is a key element in a luck-optimizing organization.

OK, but how do you hire the right people? What steps were followed at IUE? Let's walk through a typical hire for a technical person. We will show that, with only reasonable effort, you as the hiring manager can acquire the right people and enjoy the huge dividends that good hires produce.

THREE GOALS FOR HIRING

To hire well, you actually have three goals:

- Find a person with sufficient skills, knowledge, abilities, and experience to do the job. But don't stop there.

- Select someone who can contribute positively to your organization's culture.

- Make sure the new hire demonstrates a passion for doing the work you do.

The second goal deserves a closer look. You are trying to create a luck-optimized, fault-tolerant organization. So what cultural traits would you be looking for in a new hire?

You want people who think independently. Independent thinkers are self-directing (requiring less management); they create genuinely new solutions to problems; and they are self-training as needed.

You also want people who act collaboratively, people who will contribute to, and help shape, the team's understanding of what needs to be done and how best to do it. These people will distill the best solutions from the team's collective knowledge base, and they will find the best place for everyone involved in executing the solution.

Thinking independently and acting collaboratively—and the qualities they imply—are fundamental in an employee who can create value within your organization. One or the other in an individual is OK, but to optimize your luck and fault tolerance you want someone who consistently demonstrates both independent thinking and collaborative behaviors.

A word of warning: People who think independently and act collaboratively can be intimidating to those who do not. Not only do they frequently come up with the best solutions to current problems facing a working group, but they often exhibit natural leadership tendencies

LUCK-OPTIMIZING LESSON

Read any book or article on hiring, and it will likely tell you (or least imply) that the hires you make are a reflection of your character and capabilities. Isn't this one possible meaning of Ray Kroc's statement at the beginning of this chapter? The greatest limitation on your making a great hire is you. If you are not able to identify people who can think independently and act collaboratively, or if you are intimidated by such individuals, you have two options for becoming a better hiring manager than you currently are. You can

- Learn how to think independently and act collaboratively, or
- Learn to appreciate the value of people who can

around which the group spontaneously jells. Weak people in positions of responsibility may find this combination threatening.

LUCK-OPTIMIZED HIRING AND ORIENTATION

Managers and human resources professionals are frequently under tremendous pressure to fill positions immediately. Too often these days, the hiring process consists of a manager writing up a position description and filling out a position requisition and sending them to the HR department. The manager then waits for a batch of résumés to be forwarded by HR and picks the customary three "best candidates." An interview, maybe an hour long, with the hiring manager (and maybe the person at the next level up) is arranged for each applicant. Then the hiring authority picks one to hire. You may find just the person you are looking for using this method; you may also win big in Las Vegas at roulette. We prefer to stack the deck in our favor by investing the time and putting in the effort necessary to hire the right person.

Comfort with Change

Our advice: Hire people who will keep up with a rapidly changing business environment.

The method you use for matching applicants' skills and experience to your organization's needs is critical. Jobs at IUE generally had a hefty list of required skills and knowledge, but we also looked for something more, and here's why: The constant change of rapidly advancing computer technology, coupled with the demands of an aging spacecraft, meant that we needed staff who could adapt nimbly. This meant that many skills we would need in the future were not even known at the time of hire. For this reason, we also sought out people who were self-renewing—people who would continue to train themselves in new skills because that was their nature.

For instance, around fourteen years after the launch of the IUE satellite, Teays oversaw a complete overhaul of the control center hardware and software for the project's science operations. This meant converting from old, proprietary computers and software to modern workstations. He handled this transition effort largely with in-house staff, none of whom had been hired because they knew any specific language or operating system that we might use. When the time came, the staff simply built on their great computer skills and trained themselves in what they needed to know.

Meylan oversaw the introduction of the World Wide Web to the IUE Data Analysis Center. This was in the pioneering days of the Web, when few experts and little guidance were available. Once again, the in-house staff built on their skills and developed a Web-based search tool for perusing the catalog of available IUE data and having it delivered online.

How IUE Did It

Here is Teays's process for hiring a technical person, say, a resident astronomer or a telescope operator, at IUE.

Get the News Out About the Open Position

The position was advertised in our professional society's newsletter. This low-cost newsletter is specifically targeted to and read by everybody in the astronomy community who is looking for a position. There were other places to advertise, but the key was knowing where job seekers were looking. The advertisement provided contact information for the hiring manager, who also would be supervising the position. In addition to placing the ad, we encouraged the staff to use their contacts in the astronomy community to find good candidates to submit applications.

Enable Everyone to Be Part of the Process

Since this was a team environment, the people who would be working directly with the new person were an integral part of the hiring process. Chances of hiring the right person are optimized when you have experts giving you the benefit of their evaluation of the candidate. If you are trying to foster a collaborative environment, soliciting evaluations from staff is critical to making a good hire and, at the same time, reinforcing collaborative thinking and habits among team members.

After an initial screening, the candidates' résumés were placed in a secure location where the staff could examine them and make comments to the hiring manager. In the small community of professional astronomy, it was likely that some of the staff had personal knowledge of the candidates' work or knew their current boss or their college professors.

Contact References

In addition to firsthand knowledge available from the staff, we generally requested three references. We called those references! (It is amazing how many hiring horror stories begin with the fact that the references weren't actually checked.) We made certain that the person giving the reference understood the nature of the job we were looking to fill. We asked not only about the candidate's technical credentials but also about how he or she might fit personally and behaviorally into IUE's culture.

Because many young astronomers had not worked in a strong team environment, we asked about what experience the candidate had with working in a team (not mentioned in the résumé). We also asked about any missing or unclear experience and skills our staff pointed out.

Check Candidates' Other Success Venues

Many of our applicants had successful publishing records, and so we also read about their research results in the scientific literature. This provided a lot of insight into their approach to solving problems, as well as a general flavor of the quality of their work. Other fields have equivalents to publishing, such as computer programs, Web pages, designs, external program review documents, and so on, that you can examine to find out more about your candidates and their work.

Call Candidates

Next, we called the candidates. The phone interview ensured that the candidate had a detailed understanding of the nature of the job and had plenty of opportunity to ask questions. This saved time for everyone. The phone interviews were informal, but, of course, well prepared for in advance. We had a core set of questions that we asked everyone, concerning the specific characteristics of the job. We also asked about their team experience:

- Have you worked in a team environment?

- Have you served as a team leader?

- How did your team(s) achieve consensus?

Some questions, of course, varied. If candidates for a position as resident astronomer already had experience in ultraviolet astronomy, we didn't waste time asking how their research would fit in. If candidates worked in a research area unrelated to the IUE project, we asked how they saw their research interests fitting in or how they might evolve to fit in. Once again, it was not a requirement that candidates have ultraviolet astronomy experience (that is a small pool of people!), but their answers told us whether the candidates had been thinking about how compatible their experience was and how they viewed their career growth.

Meet with the Candidates

The next step was to form a short list of usually about three candidates. We then invited these finalists to the IUE project for an interview. Usually we prioritized and invited the best-qualified candidate first. If that candidate turned out to be a good fit to the job, we made the offer without interviewing the other candidates. The interview process generally occupied each candidate for an entire day. Teays, as the hiring manager, showed the candidate around and introduced him or her to the staff. He also allowed plenty of time for simply chatting in the office about the job and the candidate's interest in it. And he always set aside time for the candidate and the potential team to sit down together, *without him*, so prospects could ask candid questions about what it was like to work there.

We made it a habit to have lunch with the candidate at a local restaurant—not a fancy place meant to impress people, just a nice place to sit around the table and chat comfortably. People from the candidate's potential team were always invited to lunch as well. This gave the candidate and the staff an opportunity to interact in an informal atmosphere. Being out of the office, not in a formal interview situation, allowed people to relax and talk more freely.

Back in the office, at the end of the day, there was a final conversation to answer any questions that had cropped up during the day.

Seek Staff Reaction

Over the next day or so after the candidate's visit, Teays sought the staff's reaction. Teays, as the manager, made the final decision, but the staff had substantial input into the process and thus were supportive of the new member of the team on arrival. (Ultimate sign-off on hiring decisions came from higher levels in the organization, but the selection of candidates was pretty much left up to the immediate supervisor at IUE.)

Arrival of the New Hire

After your new employee arrives, you are responsible for seeing that his or her time isn't wasted during the first days on the job. This means spending time ensuring that the newcomer arrives to find a place to work, a computer account, a phone, and whatever else is needed to do the job. Also see that someone spends some time introducing the newcomer to people and showing him or her where things are. Once, one of us started a new job and the company hadn't even figured out where his office would be. He didn't have a computer account set up for two weeks. No one showed him where the photocopier was or how to obtain office supplies. Since he's not shy, he asked around and found these things out, but he could have been making much better use of his time. You are wasting your organization's resources if you leave the new person wandering around trying to solve these simple issues. It doesn't do much for the new employee's morale, either.

HOW HIRING PRACTICES OPTIMIZE SUCCESS

The dividends that these careful hiring practices at IUE paid were significant. They produced a workforce that was highly motivated and committed to the project. Our people always went the extra mile to get the job done, and they believed in the sanctity of doing things right. We also avoided the high cost of hiring the wrong person. Of course, we did make the occasional mistaken hire, but it was rare. It is interesting to note that the first five RAs hired by CSC at IUE either still work for CSC or retired from CSC. When CSC was bidding on subsequent contracts, it was able to document its ability to recruit and retain top-notch people.

Having a steady pool of experts allowed us to make enhancements to our products and services, using these people as project leads. It was a tremendous asset when bidding on other contracts to be able to cite these accomplishments. Additionally, consider the benefits of having such a talent pool during a crisis! Having talent in your shop allows you to throw people into the breach on short notice. This is fault tolerance in action.

Here's an example of how a gifted workforce makes a difference. A common method for pointing a satellite and keeping it stable is to use

LUCK-OPTIMIZING LESSON

Hiring employees who fit the culture and have a passion for the work also leads to lower turnover rates. Retention of experienced employees extends the return on investment in hiring and training.

gyroscopes. It takes three gyros to keep a satellite steady in all three axes. IUE was launched with six (two per axis). They failed at the rate of roughly one every two years. The staff decided that they would have a method ready for pointing the satellite with only two gyroscopes when the fourth one failed in year eight.

It failed right on time. What might have been a death blow to the mission was averted by the clever efforts of many people, but the expertise of the IUE staff was pivotal. In fact, the system they devised operated for the remainder of the mission, nearly ten years, using only the two remaining gyros and sensing equipment originally designed for totally different purposes. This example shows how making the right hires protects you from the consequences of bad luck.

Finally, let us tell you about another benefit of hiring such a staff that is not usually mentioned: It frees you as a manager to do the job of managing! If you've hired the right people you can comfortably delegate authority (see Chapter 6) without constantly having to check on progress. You are free to concentrate on things like long-range planning and hiring more good employees. Furthermore, you can actually go home at night and relax, knowing that things at work are in good hands. You can go on vacation and know that everything will be fine. Even we, chronic workaholics, were able to enjoy much-needed time off now and then.

SCREENING WITH CARE

It has become a common hiring practice in large corporations and in government agencies to develop computerized systems to match words in the résumé or other application materials to keywords in the position description. This is largely a pragmatic decision, based on the numbers of résumés that come in. Smaller businesses also may be inundated with many candidates, and quite likely only a fraction of them will be of real interest.

How do you separate the wheat from the chaff? If you don't give the applicants the kind of scrutiny we are advocating, you risk making a bad hire. If your business is small (or a small division within a larger organization), just one bad hire can create an enormous ongoing problem for you.

Currently, automated systems eliminate potentially good applicants who have not written their applications to conform to the precise terminology the computer uses in the screening process. To overcome this, you need human intervention. We know of examples, from our research on other organizations, in which applicants who had the skills and experience for a position were deemed unqualified because they didn't use the words that trigger the automated system's favorable response. In one case, unsuitable candidates' applications were passed on to the hiring manager just because they did use the right words. As difficult as it is to manage large numbers of résumés, keyword selection schemes often do not optimize success.

Some managers use the combination of résumé and job description to eliminate candidates for negative reasons rather than to select candidates for positive reasons. Of course, it is easier to eliminate candidates because of skill gaps in the résumé relative to a job description. However, if you think through the résumé more critically, you may find important reasons to favorably consider a candidate.

For example, one of us once met resistance from some staff about a potential new hire because he didn't have all the skills listed in the job description. He did have many closely related skills, seemed quite interested in the job, and had excellent references. The skeptical staff members were brought into the interview process and subsequently concluded that he probably was a good choice despite his lack of experience in a particular computer language. The new hire turned out to be a real asset immediately, largely because of his attitude and his passion for doing a good job.

These days many applicants have taken advantage of certification processes to highlight their possession of specific skills. Although such certification can be useful in the initial screening, don't take the lazy way out and use it as the only criterion for hiring. Probe deeper during the interview process to verify that the certification reflects the candidate's true skill level.

THE COSTS OF LAZY HIRING PRACTICES

Let's be blunt: If you don't have the time to work through a hiring process that gets you the right people, how are you possibly going to have time to deal with all the misfits you end up with?

One of the biggest headaches we have seen is hiring someone who has the precise list of skills needed for the job, but who doesn't fit your culture. Hiring someone with strong technical skills but incompatible social behaviors might work under some circumstances, but it is hardly going to work in a strong team environment. (We've seen this experiment conducted; it isn't pretty.) You may encounter someone who would make an outstanding employee for some other shop but doesn't fit your culture. IUE occasionally, especially in the early years, hired excellent astronomers who wanted to spend more time on research and less on service to the community than was envisioned by NASA. They were capable enough, but the fit wasn't quite right, so they moved on to other places (with goodwill and a good endorsement from the IUE management).

Sometimes you are under pressure to hire quickly to fill an open slot. Or you may be hiring someone who will be a consultant or a subcontractor in another organization's workforce, and the customer organization has influence over the hire. Consider one of our post-IUE cases where both conditions held. Art (not his real name) did not think that Lee (ditto), the candidate, would fit the culture or had a passion for doing the work. Nevertheless, the prime contractor wanted Lee, who was hired against Art's better judgment, by Art's boss, who was trying to keep the customer happy. In a fairly short while they had to fire Lee, and the whole affair proved to be a huge embarrassment. The prime contractor blamed Art's company, rather than remembering that they themselves were the ones who had pushed for hiring Lee.

If you don't have adequate influence over the hiring process, or agreement with those who do, your ability to optimize your luck in hiring will be reduced. In those cases, you must accept that your ability to build the team you need will be compromised.

If your hiring process is defined at the corporate level and it's any good, it will serve as a guide that helps your managers build hiring habits that lead to the acquisition of better and better talent. Always remember, creating luck-optimizing hiring habits will help you build a stronger business culture.

TIME FOR CAREFUL HIRING

If you and your staff spend more time on hiring a new employee, won't you also spend more money? Studies by human resources professionals have shown that if you make a poor choice in a hire and have to replace that person eventually, it can cost you big time. Estimates of this cost are different for various industries, but they are particularly high for exempt technical positions, ranging as high as 100 to 150 percent of the employee's annual salary. And, if you have ever been involved in the long and painful process of firing a poorly performing employee, then you will know that smart hiring is cheap insurance. (Take a look at the Society for Human Resource Management Web site, at www.shrm.org., for more information.)

Suppose you decide to train your poor hire. How much time, money, and effort do you think is reasonable to invest in the attempt? If you succeed in turning the bad employee around, you've still added to

LUCK-OPTIMIZING LESSON

You may say you're not hiring stargazers, but this still applies to you. Of course, you won't use exactly the same hiring process we did at IUE. You will adapt it to your organization and its culture. Teays adapted his hiring procedures at his later jobs, adjusting to the culture and nature of the work, but he continued to follow the same underlying principles. Your organization may have more specific and rigid procedures for hiring. If, however, your organization's hiring process doesn't allow you to put the necessary amount of care into the process, seriously consider reengineering it. Whatever your process does, it needs to identify candidates who have

- The ability to do the job
- A passion for doing the job
- Whatever it takes to do the job effectively within your corporate culture

your hiring cost. If you don't suceed, you have merely thrown good money after bad.

Perhaps you feel that you just have to keep all positions filled; you don't need, nor can you afford, to wait for the best. But this is a panic response, and it will not help you develop a great, enduring, organization. It is not a fault-tolerant practice. Consider hiring temporary help or outsourcing to another organization until you find the right person.

You may have realized you are not a great judge of people. One advantage of involving your team in the hiring process is that you gain a broader insight, which gives you a better chance to come to a good decision. You may discover that someone on your team is especially good at picking superior candidates, and so you have someone whose advice you can rely on—and someone to keep an eye on for possible recruiting into management ranks.

Particularly difficult in these times is the threat of litigation with respect to the hiring (and firing) process. Your organization may have created restrictive hiring policies as a result of employment law, experience, or horror stories from the industry. Look at what we are suggesting and work out what you think you should do to get the people you need. Then sit down with your human resources representative and talk it over. See where you are constrained—and where you can make adjustments that give you a process leading to successful hiring.

As a hiring manager, you want to form a set of hiring habits that helps you build the strongest possible team. Others will pick up your habits, which ultimately strengthens the effectiveness of your corporate culture.

DELEGATION

Few things can help an individual more than to place responsibility on him, and to let him know you trust him.

BOOKER T. WASHINGTON, EDUCATOR

According to IUE managers, once you've hired the right people, you need to *let them do their job*. Primarily, this is about the power of delegation. Were we New Age, spiritual types, we'd call this the "power of letting go." But we're not. Delegation is vastly more aggressive than that. It is the skill of multiplying your strengths by applying the strengths of others to your goals and objectives.

Delegation is the most empowering behavior you as a manager can exercise. This is not merely because it empowers your people. It also empowers you. It empowers your organization, too, because when you delegate you exhibit the kinds of managerial habits that need to suffuse every part of your business.

That's an important point. Most business writers speak of delegation as empowering workers. But that's only part of the story. Delegation is also important because of the power it generates in the hands of the person who knows how to use it constructively.

We absolutely love delegation. Why? Because with a suitable team (since we've hired the right people, as described in Chapter 5) we can do the work of scores of people.

Our post-IUE experience showed us two things about delegation. When we went about our usual practice of delegation with teams we inherited, we were able to improve the teams' business value by half again to double. That's pretty good. However, when we formed our own teams, we were typically able to generate fives times the business value compared to other teams tasked with similar objectives. This wasn't merely because we picked better people. It was because of a greater mutual understanding about the use of delegation between us and the team members we selected.

DELEGATION AT IUE

By the time we got to the International Ultraviolet Explorer project the habits of delegation were firmly entrenched in the culture. This was one of the primary reasons we interviewed all the managers present at the formation of the project. We wanted to determine how these practices were instigated.

Recall that NASA's person in charge at the beginning, Al Boggess, knew Charlie Wu, Al Holm, and Skip Schiffer and connected them with CSC, which had the science operations contract. Boggess then cut the three scientists loose to make satellite operations work. Boggess became a facilitator of the mission he wanted to see built. Consider the power this delegating generated for Boggess. He was literally able to create something from nothing. Once he got approval to put the project together, Boggess gave the contractors freedom to flesh out his vision. In a short time, developments for IUE were up and running well. This was the start of the corporate culture habit of delegation at the IUE project. Yoji Kondo, when he took over from Boggess, continued the practice. As Kondo says, "Unless you can trust people, you can't get trusted."

Once methods and procedures were established, new hires onto the IUE project were given a great deal of individual responsibility in fairly short order. The telescope operators and the resident astronomers had a formal training period of three months, after which they were responsible for operating the satellite. They were typically recent graduates or, at most, had been working for a year or two before coming to IUE. After the training period a team of one TO and one RA was in charge of running the science operations—maneuvering the satellite, acquiring the targets, collecting the data, controlling the scientific instruments, ensuring the safety of the hardware, downloading the data, and monitoring the health of the satellite.

The continuous operation of the satellite coupled with Earth's motion around the sun meant the starting times of observing shifts changed by two hours each month. This frequently put shifts in the middle of the night, when the TO and the RA were counted on to make the right decisions to balance scientific return and satellite safety. This was serious responsibility delegated to relatively junior personnel, especially during times when IUE was NASA's only operating orbital observatory. Everyone was concerned about the possibility of damaging a $500 million national investment. So, everyone, especially the bright young freshouts, appreciated the trust implied by this delegated responsibility.

Earlier we related the story of rebuilding the satellite operations system. Teays delegated this effort to a senior staff member. Teays's only role was to provide the staffer with needed resources or technical advice. This allowed Teays the freedom to concentrate on his other duties.

In another example, Teays delegated to a two-person team the task of developing a user-friendly interface for displaying and navigating a collection of databases with information about stars. This would simplify many aspects of IUE's satellite operations and improve services to guest observers. (Remember, this was during a time when graphical user interfaces were still in their infancy.) Left to themselves, these two people developed an outstanding package that was integrated into the IUE ground control system. Other NASA spacecraft missions requested copies, and it became a very popular package.

There are times, of course, when things go wrong even in a good team. At one point, serious questions were raised about the quality and integrity of a prototype system that was being designed to supersede the

LUCK-OPTIMIZING
LESSON

Delegation needs to be conducted in the open. This facilitates the spread of knowledge about what the company is up to and who is capable of making specific kinds of contributions. Increasingly, most of the work of figuring out whom to delegate tasks to at the meeting will be done by your staff rather than by you. One reason this works is that a culture of delegation distributes the responsibility in such a way that the staff embraces the success of the organization as their own.

IUE project's original data processing software. Customers indicated that they did not trust the new software, and they were threatening to pull the plug on funding needed to finish the prototype. Obviously, this was a serious issue!

The CSC Director of Science Programs delegated investigation of this issue to Teays. If there was a problem, Teays needed to fix it. If there was no problem, he needed to recapture customer confidence. Upper management's trust, backed by carte blanche to tap CSC resources, motivated Teays to work even harder than usual. As it happened, the software did exactly what it was supposed to do, and everything turned out fine.

DELEGATION IN A LUCK-OPTIMIZED SYSTEM

Delegating a task to someone is not an isolated event. Delegation is an integral part of planning and operations. For example, following a team meeting, everyone should have a clear picture of who is responsible for what.

With time, your team will become familiar with the process of delegation and with the broader, interlocking needs of the organization. As a result they will be better equipped to identify opportunities and threats. They will be more prepared to respond quickly and appropriately, without asking the chain of command for advice. Their rapid responses to opportunities optimize your luck, just as their rapid responses to crises optimize your fault tolerance.

Our experience at IUE and later in private sector consulting demonstrated that widespread delegation produces awareness in your team about the collective abilities of the team members. When someone becomes responsible for a task, he or she learns quickly how to identify teammates with experience or knowledge that can be brought to bear on the task. In addition, the team's confidence in their ability to meet new challenges grows with the successful completion of each delegated task. This creates and strengthens a group of collaborative partners, people who see each other as proven performers.

STEPS FOR LEARNING TO DELEGATE

A couple of things have to be in place before good delegation can occur. First, you have to hire the right people—right in terms of being able to contribute to business progress and success and in fitting into the culture. Second, you have to observe these people to obtain, in your mind, an accurate profile of their skill sets.

Remember one of the chief goals of any manager: You want your actions and the actions of your team to optimize your chances of success. Don't think of people as merely filling slots; such thinking is lazy management, plain and simple. Think of even the people operating in the most menial of functions as multifaceted resources. This not only elevates their dignity but also helps you draw more out of them than mere labor. If they've been at the job a long time, their experience can be an important guide to better ways of doing things.

This leaves one last act. You have to actually delegate a responsibility to someone. Here are the steps for getting started:

1. Define the scope of the task. In a small team, the manager may be able to do this alone. In a larger team, with a wide range of activities, you may want to consult with senior staff members to provide needed details.

2. Select a person who seems to have the skills required for the task.

3. Spell out the responsibility as clearly as you can.

4. Set your expectations of *what* you want done (not *how* you want it done) in concrete terms.

5. Set a time when you want the task finished.

6. Cut the person loose to do it.

7. Remain in the background as a willing resource, if needed.

By following these steps you get at least two kinds of payoff. First, you can assess how well you delegate (select a person, assign a task, and support that person through the completion of the assigned task). Other things to consider:

- If the person you chose succeeds, both of you have learned more about your capabilities.

- If the person achieves a qualified success, then you can determine whether you perhaps didn't select the best person or whether you weren't clear enough about the assignment.

- If the person isn't successful at all, then you have some tough questions to answer—about the process you used to delegate the responsibility, how you chose the person, how well you described what you wanted done, and so on.

Second, getting put in charge of a small project allows people to show what they can do, and their performance gives their manager concrete data on the way each was able to perform. This is a key technique for identifying people who are ready to take on larger responsibilities (see Chapter 10 on recognizing and rewarding success on the job). This also gives employees a chance to try their wings and to find out if they like taking on a leadership role. This practice worked so well at the IUE project that managers were almost always promoted from within.

Learning how to delegate is an iterative process: You have to practice delegating to get good at it. If things don't go particularly well the first couple of times, ask yourself:

- Did you understand the task well enough to know what abilities were really needed?

- Were you familiar enough with the person you chose to be sure you matched the right person to the task?

- Did you understand the task well enough to communicate accurately what needed to be done?

- Did you communicate with sufficient detail what you wanted done (not how you wanted it done)?

- Did you make it clear when you wanted the task completed?

- Did you give the person the autonomy and authority to accomplish the task without your help or interference?

- When the person did need assistance, were you able to provide mentoring through to success? Without taking over?

Successful managers are always assessing their approaches to things. No one ever knows enough about delegation to take delegation skills for granted.

Delegation is important throughout your managerial career. It's a vital habit to develop when you're just starting out and you're not used to having someone else do your work. You may be tempted to take the work back and do it yourself. Resist that temptation. Why? Because you are learning a new set of skills as a manager in a people-based, luck-optimizing system. Delegation allows you to build larger, more intricate, systems and processes that handle a more comprehensive range of business conditions.

REWARDS OF DELEGATION

From the manager's standpoint, perhaps the most rewarding experience is coming in to work in the morning, getting a report that the crew had a problem during the night, and then getting the details on how they fixed it. No wake-up call to the manager. No one wondering what to do until morning. The crew simply diagnosed the problem and took care of it. At the IUE project, our reports to CSC and NASA management often cited these kinds of incidents and solutions. Successful delegation allows both team and manager to demonstrate just how good they are on a regular basis.

Another dividend of effective delegation is the peace of mind it grants to the manager. If you have delegated effectively to competent people, then you can attend off-site business functions or even take vacations without worrying about what's going on back at the office.

Some organizations are run by people who do not understand the functions and uses of delegation. For example, Teays worked in a company where managers of other departments had a hard time accepting the fact that, when he was out of town, his deputy was empowered to make decisions and participate in management meetings in his stead. They wanted to wait until Teays returned to discuss anything sensitive or important. It took some training of his peers to get them to understand that he was completely serious about delegating to and trusting his deputy to handle things.

RISKS OF DELEGATION

Why do so many managers seem to lack appreciation for the dividends of delegating to good people and letting them do their jobs? Why don't they delegate effectively? Perhaps the dividends need to be spelled out in a different way. Or perhaps other habits in the corporate culture make delegation a high-risk behavior for managers.

- If you haven't hired the right people, delegation could be risky. It might not pay off. There would be no dividend.

- If the corporate culture doesn't include a belief in the sanctity of doing things right, there would probably be few, if any, habits of real value in your culture. If your team doesn't believe in doing things right, delegation could be risky. It might not pay off. There would be no dividend.

- If your organization is not fault tolerant, any mistake becomes a disaster because you don't have a network of productive habits in place to repair damage. If mistakes habitually become disasters, and your people habitually make mistakes, delegation could be risky. It might not pay off. There would be no dividend.

- If top management habitually creates fear or indecision within the managerial structure, you might be afraid to make any decisions; so, delegation could be risky. It might not pay off. There would be no dividend.

If your company's culture includes ineffective or detrimental habits of communication, then you might not be confident that you have made your delegated wishes clear. You also might not believe that you will get updates about your delegated tasks and therefore won't have any knowledge of their status. That would feel risky, wouldn't it? You might never even know whether you succeeded. You wouldn't know if your delegation paid off. You wouldn't know if you secured a dividend or not.

If you're working in that kind of culture, it's no wonder you won't delegate!

EXAMPLES OF SUCCESS IN DELEGATION

In his post-IUE managerial and consulting experience, Meylan has yet to deliver the same types of services more than once. Every job or engagement has been in a different industry or service area.

In cases where your business context is unfamiliar and the territory unknown, you can (and should) continue the IUE practice, which in these cases translates to

- Finding the people who know what they are doing here and

- Letting them do their job, or

- Expanding their responsibilities to accelerate progress

In other words, you have to dig in fast and find your crack team of local subject matter experts.

One of Meylan's clients in the insurance industry called him in to fix a surprise problem. A Y2K project had just discovered that 25 percent of its mainframe software library had been missed during its library audit three years earlier. Correcting this oversight was urgent because *all* remediation for Y2K fixes was due to be implemented in three months. The client had spent three years on the other 75 percent, so people there estimated another year of work. But the new fixes had to be finished and delivered for acceptance testing in four weeks. In an effort to speed up the process, the client gave Meylan half of the code and its main Y2K contractor the other half.

The client authorized Meylan to call in anyone he wanted, so he gathered up the in-house experts and they met with the people who had long-term ownership of the various library segments. "Each of you has three weeks to get your part of the library fixed," Meylan told them. "So get to work. We'll have an update meeting each week until we're done. If you run into trouble and you don't think you can make your deadline, let me know as soon as possible so we can get you additional help. If you need any technical tools, let me know about that as well. And then let me know when you've finished your code so I can pass it down to the testing and acceptance teams."

They got the work done in two weeks, which gave the testers even more time to check it out. And it was perfect.

The team working on the other half of the code, the hired experts on Y2K remediation, missed the deadline. Maybe they got the harder code. Maybe their managers didn't delegate effectively. Or maybe they really didn't know what they were doing.

For his part, Meylan made the assignments, gave them to the right people, and communicated expectations clearly. The project was completed ahead of schedule. And Meylan slept well every night.

Meylan had a similar experience designing and constructing a customer support center for a major telephone company getting into the Internet services business. He had to integrate a system with machines he'd never heard of, using dubious software technologies, employing upbeat people who were technically mediocre by IUE project standards.

Eventually, a few stars began to appear, and Meylan was able to get enough of their time to build a team that could learn for him. The more they learned, the more responsibility he gave them. After three months, Meylan had three solid lieutenants, one handling call center technologies, one handling Web-based technologies, and one handling wide area network technologies. Another small group was handling support personnel training. After four months he had a prototype customer support center up and running, and after nine months he cut over to a fully automated call center with all the bells and whistles.

EXAMPLES OF FAILURE TO DELEGATE

Almost everyone has seen the consequences of poor or failed delegation. One of us once worked for an entrepreneur who had started and then sold a successful company several years earlier. As sometimes happens, she'd enjoyed a run of beginner's luck—she'd been in the right place at the right time with her first venture. However, that's not the way she saw it. In her new start-up, she acted as if she were the only person on her staff who understood how to get a successful company off the ground, as well as the only subject matter expert.

What was frustrating was that she actually did hire the right people, but she couldn't leave them alone to do their job. There was some serious talent on her team. She hired great software designers, software engineers, and businesspeople to push the products out into the market. Unable to use their skills to advantage, these bright people departed after a short time, leaving the business incapable of delivering on projects for lack of human resources.

In another case Meylan had to placate a bored and restless team of Y2K consultants who were planning to quit en masse. Their complaint was that the customer's system-level policies made it impossible for them to do their jobs: By policy, outside personnel weren't allowed to service the computers. This company had hired consultants that, by policy, it couldn't use—at a cost of $500,000 a month! Since the customer wouldn't delegate tasks to the consultants, Meylan delegated training tasks to them, based on the customer's systems, that furthered their professional development and that might eventually be useful to his client.

Consider another example: a work unit in a federal agency where the employees were required, every day, to fill out a form indicating that they had complied with standard practices for handling files and similar tasks that day. They had to certify each day that they had done their jobs properly! If the employees weren't trusted to do their jobs, how could they be trusted to fill out the form?

INNER STRENGTH—
THE CORNERSTONE OF DELEGATION

Most effective leaders would agree that the ability to delegate stems from and requires inner strength.

Two important keys help you develop this inner strength. First, you must be willing to trust people to accomplish their delegated tasks. Without trust, delegation doesn't happen. What you get instead is the making of assignments that you then either micromanage or snatch back to do yourself.

And that brings us back to hiring the right people. At the IUE project, candidates for open positions had to be able to generate faith in their trustworthiness. Over the course of the mission's lifetime those characteristics became easy to identify because we practiced watching for them. As a result, we had a whole project full of trustworthy people, which made delegating a natural part of the project's culture.

Second, you need confidence in yourself to develop the inner strength necessary to successfully delegate. Do you believe that good people make you look good, or that they make you look bad? Without confidence you will view life as an unending series of rivalries.

There was a lot of brainpower on the IUE project. There had to be. It was a space-based orbiting observatory meeting the demands of thousands of scientists. Most people came to the project with exceptional skills and abilities—and a lot of self-confidence! We had a few egotists,

LUCK-OPTIMIZING LESSON

The productive aspects of delegation can become motivators for you if you keep them in mind. Delegation is

- A vital component of a comprehensive risk reduction strategy
- An effective corporate communication habit
- A promoter of the sanctity of doing things right
- A promoter of trust throughout the organization
- A network of productive habits that generates a fault-tolerant organization
- The heart of a strong, cross-trained, team

and we also had a few insecure individuals. But, for the most part, the project staff were confident, competent, pleased, and proud to be doing what they were doing.

You have to find it in yourself to succeed as a manager. You have to find it in others, too, if you want to move them into management. Creating new managers is the most critical form of delegation. You have to have confidence in yourself to delegate management effectively. Eventually, you reach a point where you admire and respect superior talent, not fear it.

ADAPTABILITY

If change inside your company is slower than the change outside your company, the end is in sight.

JACK WELCH, FORMER CEO, GENERAL ELECTRIC

Everything about your business environment is continuously changing. Consistently succeeding under continuously changing conditions requires the use of luck-optimizing and fault-tolerant systems. These types of systems are explicitly designed to engage with changing conditions to your business's best advantage. You use them to build and, when necessary, to rebuild your personal habits of success, as well as the methods and procedures of your business. In other words, you use luck-optimizing and fault-tolerant systems to *adapt*. If you forecast or encounter a change in the business environment that your current habits or processes can't handle, you need to build new responses quickly. If the change is potentially positive, you want your luck-optimizing processes to kick in. Conversely, if the change is potentially damaging, you want your fault-tolerant safeguards to switch on.

Managers of the International Ultraviolet Explorer project were adaptable because they took a luck-optimizing approach to handling their responsibilities. In the next section we outline the steps that create adaptability and demonstrate how each step works.

FOUR STEPS TO ADAPTABILITY

You can't have efficient business operations if everyone is busy figuring out how to do things fresh every day. Having in place habits based on effective methods and procedures is vital to efficiency and profitability. But when conditions change, as they frequently did for the IUE project, some habits may need to be suspended until a new best practice can be established. The faster you can adapt behaviors to the new conditions and establish new habits, the stronger your competitive advantage.

Fortunately, human beings are adept at acquiring new skills and turning them into habits each time their environment changes. We call this the "master process of continuous habit management," which is composed of four steps:

1. Remain continuously observant of your surroundings and alert to environmental changes.

2. Continue trying new things until you get the results you want.

3. Convert successful behaviors into personal habits and corporate procedures to save response time to future changes.

4. Discard obsolete habits when your continuous observation tells you it's time to create new ones.

This process helps you deal with the ongoing tension between habits and adaptability. Adhering to habits is vital to efficiency as long as your environment changes little. However, when things in your environment have changed to the point where your habits are a detriment, you have to reformulate your behaviors to succeed under the new conditions.

Step 1: Be Observant

Most workers are so focused on their assigned tasks that they notice very little of what goes on around them. How did we lose track of our powers of observation?

Two things seem to explain this. First, the typical work environment is extremely safe compared to the natural environment. Most workers don't have to watch for life-threatening predators or hunt for their next meal. Second, success on the job requires us to focus on a relatively narrow and constant set of behaviors. During our education many of us are taught to eliminate distractions so we can concentrate on our studies. This carries over into our work routines. We learn to either eliminate distractions or ignore anything that doesn't pertain to the task at hand.

Learning to study well does not kill our powers of observation. However, it may result in a luck-limiting habit. While we may develop skill in deriving knowledge from documents, we may lose the ability to develop knowledge directly from our surroundings.

There are only two reasons you would need to adapt anything you're already doing:

- The environment has changed, so you need to do different things.

- You want to get more out of your environment than you already do.

In either case, you will need to keep your eyes open—be observant—and so will everyone on your team if you are to create the behavioral changes you and your organization need to make.

Step 2: Try New Things

Innovation is vital in responding to new observations about market trends. Innovation also can create market trends if the product or service meets a compelling human or business need.

IUE project scientist Yoji Kondo told us, "Business is an empirical process. You're always testing against results." (The words *empirical* and *testing* are science-speak for "observing and experimenting in the real world," as opposed to working from "the hypothetical.") IUE staff and managers were continually looking for ways to squeeze more observing time and data out of the satellite, more out of the data products, and more out of the community being served by the project.

One of the main reasons for this extra effort was competition for funding with other NASA astronomy projects. Some sponsors of other projects even went so far as to single out IUE as an old project that should be cut, and its funding used elsewhere. So we had to stay on our toes. We had to keep improving the way we did everything, from inventing advanced scheduling methods for satellite observations to creating some of the first e-commerce solutions for delivery of data products and software tools. Innovation became our mainstay. And we were good at it.

It would be overstating the case to maintain that NASA needed IUE to make its other astronomy projects work well, but it's safe to say that there was extensive knowledge transfer from IUE to other NASA projects. Newer projects often were not able to live up to the standards of productivity set by IUE, and as a result many of them began adopting or adapting IUE procedures to improve their performance. IUE pioneered the methods and procedures that made other missions, such as the Hubble Space Telescope, successful. But then, many of the operational people working on the Hubble Space Telescope are former IUE employees.

Step 3: Convert Successful Behaviors into Habits and Procedures

This is where personal flexibility is perhaps the most critical. Such flexibility facilitates the replacement of obsolete habits with new habits dictated by your continuous observations. Everyone should assume that all methods and procedures are provisional. That is, they are important only so long as they meet daily business challenges. Here are some thoughts from our IUE peer Rich Arquilla, after reading some early notes for this book.

> I was also struck . . . where you have, for instance, flexibility in response to real-time situations. The reason that struck me is that it sort of hit a chord with what I have seen over the years.
>
> What you are describing there is sort of a tactical flexibility, the flexibility to deal with the problems in the short term. That is important especially in spacecraft operations. It is vital where unexpected problems can come up. The second thing that you have mentioned here,

adaptability from a strategic response standpoint . . . is the harder thing to get. I have seen situations . . . where you have people who are trained to be tactically flexible. I mean they will respond to a particular request, they will respond to a particular situation by applying things they've always known, to solve the problem. But if you tell them, "OK, now we're going to change [how you do things]. You need to change it for various reasons, either because it's becoming outdated or it is no longer going to deal with the problems that we expect to encounter," that is a much harder thing to do. A lot of times people have a lot of resistance to that. People are resistant to change. People who have been doing things for a long time will resist changing those familiar techniques and procedures. The reason that it comes to mind with IUE is that we did have to change our ground system. And we did it. In our case I think that it made it easier, because we were all debating about selling tickets to smash the old equipment . . . because it was so difficult to work with. That really was an impressive achievement if you think about it. We did that in house. We actually created an updated new ground system for the project. And it did make a difference. I think that we did extend the mission.

Why is procedural change so emotionally difficult for so many people? We suspect that this difficulty relates closely to the same factors that diminish people's habits of observation. Suppose a given workforce hasn't been observing the business world around them. Suppose further that you haven't been keeping them informed of the changing conditions affecting your business. Now you come along and, for perfectly good reasons, force a change of procedures on them. Are they going to be happy about that? Of course not.

They aren't going to be happy about it because they don't see the need for change. Their habitual behaviors up to this point have been perfectly sufficient for meeting their personal employment goals and for accomplishing their job. Furthermore, this change represents a potential threat to the workforce for any of the following reasons:

- The new procedures might be too hard to learn. Then the workers face being fired and replaced by younger people who are less expensive to employ and perhaps more able to learn.

- The new procedures might not work. They might be bad, faulty, or dangerous, but management might not see it that way. Then the workers face being fired because the work can't be done.

- The new methods might work just fine—and require only half the people to do the same amount of work as before. Then the workers face being laid off because there is now nothing for them to do.

- The employees, having experienced many grand changes that didn't really change anything, might lack motivation to adopt the new procedures, since the idea will blow over in a short while. Then they face being fired because of their seeming obstinance.

So what is the solution? If managers kept their employees informed about the business and its environment, many changes would make sense to workers. Workers can help you build luck-optimizing and fault-tolerant methods and procedures when they know what's going on. Keeping channels of communication open not only motivates people, it fuels their creativity so they can help build the new solutions needed to keep the organization strong and agile.

Many people find innovation fun and exciting if they are closely involved in what's going on. IUE staffers often suggested changes to management. They might have encountered a problem with an existing procedure and started experimenting with possible solutions. After they nailed down the new solution, they'd offer it up to their manager for feedback and consideration. This freedom to explore improvements meant that a constant flow of fresh ideas was always pouring in.

When it's widely known that management desires and implements innovation, change nearly becomes a nonissue.

Step 4: Discard Obsolete Habits

If you want to divest your organization of obsolete habits, you need to ensure effective training in and appropriate reinforcement and reward for the needed new procedures and behaviors. Don't leave any opportunity or payoff for people to use the old habits.

LUCK-OPTIMIZING LESSON

People persist in old habits for as long as they pay off. Extinguishing habits that have become a sink of time and money for your business can be difficult. You have to run the communication campaign to educate people effectively about changes. Design training to transmit new skills and achieve buy-in. And be sure to remove every possible form of payoff that these habits could still deliver to someone.

In business, if you're keeping up with your market, your personal habits and your company's procedures are evolving naturally. You and your team are busy using up-to-date practices, so you don't have time to use the old, underperforming ones.

Keep in mind that we're presuming an organization where the workforce is being educated by management about the state of the business's affairs. This sharing of information can effectively motivate the needed changes in an honest, peer-to-peer way. We're not advocating that the top person take a dictatorial approach to this. We're trying to build luck-optimizing and fault-tolerant systems. The reasons for change need to be communicated to the staff if for no other reason than that it demonstrates clear respect for your team. That buys a lot of goodwill in most cases.

Good changes designed for legitimate business reasons (such as the growth of the business or survival in tough circumstances) must include the execution of enterprise-wide communication about them. It's up to leadership to make sure that team members know in advance why change is coming. This is critical to facilitate employees' readiness and willingness to perform their redesigned tasks to win in the new business context.

BUSINESS WORLD EXPERIENCES
WITH ADAPTABILITY

In Chapter 6, we mentioned a group of consultants getting ready to leave a major Y2K job. How did Meylan avert the walkout? First, he offered a reality check: "You're COBOL programmers, and you're never going to see these hourly pay rates again once the Y2K rush is over. We don't know why they've hired you and then left you idle. All we know for sure is that they want you here." Second, he kept his approach constructive: "Study their system as deeply as you can, and if they release work to us, we'll be ready. In addition to that, study related technologies in case they need something more advanced than Y2K remediation. Let me repeat: they want us here for a reason. We just haven't been able to figure it out yet." In other words, study other programming languages that the customer might be able to use. Study Web enablement on mainframe computers. The customer might ask for something unexpected and you'll be ready to deliver! Use an adaptive approach to unsatisfactory work conditions to prepare for when the conditions change.

At the ISP start-up mentioned in Chapter 3, the game plan for entering the market changed every three to five days. While this might not be a problem for three guys working out of a garage, it's a bit of a tussle for a major company with two hundred people committed to the launch. The managers would either be refocusing who the target customers were, or which technologies to sell, or how to position themselves against AOL or some other rising ISP star. In other words, the management team was constantly attempting to find their most likely winning strategy and adapt to it.

Meylan and his customer were tasked with building customer support. The customer had solid experience in call center development and he had certain adaptive strategies he could employ to get his job done while satisfying his "moving target" CEO. One of the customer's strategies was to buffer his team against "changes in the managerial wind." The group kept on target with the technology buildouts and call center representative training, and Meylan's customer changed a few key slides in his standard PowerPoint presentation when needed to show how customer support would be able to meet the challenges posed by the new directives.

Meylan's customer usually spent no more than an hour on each wild turn of managerial directive. That in turn kept Meylan available to direct key activities in the fabrication of a truly world-class customer support system. He didn't get bent out of shape. He didn't whine about having to redirect massive amounts of effort. Instead, he kept his cool, formulated his message to the CEO, and stayed on the path to success. He used his adaptive strategy to deal effectively with changes in executive direction, keep his technical team on target, and save a lot of time by applying his experience in dealing with change. And it worked!

THE PAYOFF OF BEING ADAPTABLE

Adaptability confers survivability. That's the primary payoff. When things change, you have to be able to succeed under the new conditions. But there's a second payoff. That's where your adaptive skills go beyond survivability and on to an embarrassment of riches. By rights, the IUE project should have ended in its eighth year of operation. Adaptability bought it another ten years of strong success, more than doubling its productive lifetime.

Taking an adaptable approach to things involves being able to broaden your perspective. Even something that might seem as autocratic or unilaterally determined as decision making will usually be more effective if the need to be adaptable is built into the process. Barry Turnrose had the following to say about decision making at IUE:

> You know, to my recollection it wasn't particularly autocratic either. You could be decisive without being totally autocratic. . . . [It was] not exactly that everything was done by consensus, but it wasn't done by a method that seemed to be just fiat, that made no sense to anybody. Nor because it said in a rule book of management that . . . you have to do things this way. . . . It seemed to just be natural and reasonable.

LUCK-OPTIMIZING LESSON

Human adaptability has always derived from experimentation—that is, from research and development. Research and development is where you mine for serendipity, those unanticipated discoveries that completely change the current situation. Adaptability has always been about innovation, solution building, testing and retesting. Further, especially in the case of serendipity, new discoveries go to waste if the discoverers aren't willing to flow with what their discoveries suggest.

This approach to decision making remained pervasive throughout the project's lifetime. While it sounds pretty loose, in practice it boiled down to a communal sorting of the facts coupled with a melding of ideas leading to best possible responses. It didn't matter whether the change we had to deal with was good or bad. We simply had to find out what we could about the change and respond in the most constructive manner.

Human adaptability is a cerebral approach to the challenges of life, survival, or business. You beat the environment, or you beat the competition in your environment, by applying brainpower more effectively than you did before, or more effectively than your competition does.

Personal and organizational adaptability, from the beginning of human existence, has always been about luck optimization and fault tolerance.

RUNNING LEAN

We have always found that people are most productive in small teams with tight budgets, time lines, and the freedom to solve their own problems.

JOHN ROLLWAGEN, FORMER CEO, CRAY RESEARCH

If you have never experienced lean times, then you may not be prepared to deal with them when they appear. Knowing how to operate in a lean environment is an excellent fault-tolerance mechanism.

THE PEOPLE FACTOR

If you've been thinking that we yammer too much about hiring the right people, here's why we've been so persistent with that message.

If you've hired people who can think independently and act collaboratively, you have a team that will step up to the challenges of being slightly understaffed. In this case, running lean is a good thing. It is fiscally efficient and an automatic team-building condition. Running lean is in many respects the "mother of invention" for your business. It will result in better business processes as well as better products and services.

If instead you have hired people who need to be led around at every turn or who operate in competitive or adversarial ways, you'll find that running lean is a bad thing. No one will take the initiative to create needed solutions for your company or your customers. Team members will grumble that the situation is suboptimal and question how you expect to accomplish anything with your business. Blame and accusations about tactical and strategic failures will proliferate. Running lean when you haven't hired the right people will probably lead to business failure.

Lean staffing means employees are fully engaged; they don't have time to sit around idle. This pays a number of dividends, the most important of which is that a lean organization is driven to be collaborative. We've discussed several examples where the IUE staff managed to apply new technology to enhance productivity, using largely in-house employees. In a lean organization you are compelled to share people among departments to meet the organization's needs. This promotes a broader understanding of the entire organization and creates a de facto process for cross-training. The lean organization is led to these luck-optimizing approaches out of necessity. A collaborative work environment is supported by working lean, and at the same time, running lean requires collaboration.

In the opposite case—where you haven't hired well—you need a surplus of employees to make up for the effort wasted on competitive behavior and other habits aimed at targets other than your business's success.

Maybe you're thinking, "Shouldn't we all strive to have a surplus of resources at hand to run our business?" Not necessarily. Running lean is fault tolerant. Working with surplus is not. If your processes and culture rely on an opulent flow of funds into your organization, you are probably not prepared to deal with financial reversals. Remember all the dot-coms that, a few years ago, got handed millions of dollars at a throw? Some of them tried to build a real business with all that venture capital, but a lot of them pampered themselves despite a lack of real results. "We work hard, so we're going to play hard," they told the business press. Previous generations had more of a "We're going to work hard until we consistently clear a profit from operations; we can play when we retire" approach. If revenue isn't rolling in, or if expenses are greater than revenue, you need to dole out those extravagant resources carefully to ensure that you will make it to the finish line with a business success on your hands. Where are those dot-coms now? Most of them crashed and burned.

When we talk about running lean we are not advocating eliminating employee benefits to reduce operating costs. That would jeopardize your chances of recruiting and retaining the right people. We are not suggesting that you not invest in employee training or new technology. That would not help your organization remain agile and optimize its chances of survival in the future. You must spend the money on the resources you need to accomplish your organization's mission. Your spending decisions should be based on meeting those goals over the long haul.

RUNNING LEAN AT IUE

The senior manager who controlled IUE's budget at NASA headquarters was once asked at a meeting about the project's low funding levels. He replied, "IUE has traditionally been underfunded. And it will continue to be underfunded." In fact, when managers of later missions were arguing for larger budgets, they frequently had IUE thrown in their faces. "If IUE can do it that cheaply, why can't you?" Let's look at a few examples from IUE to clarify the points we have made about running lean.

Staffing

IUE ran extremely lean on people in the beginning. The level of effort needed was poorly understood, and staffing was built on that poorly understood model. That staffing level was too lean, and steps were taken to correct it during the course of the mission. However, the systemic short-handedness created a resilient mutual reliance within the project team. We always had to stretch a bit to get the job done. There wasn't room for deadwood. We were watching each other from inside the same fishbowl. Accountability and visibility worked hand in hand to create very effective workers.

Office Space

Minimal office space was allotted to the IUE project. The government allocates office space based on the number of civil servants employed on a project, but IUE used contractors, who didn't figure in the head count, almost exclusively. Eventually, CSC acquired office space off site, near Goddard Space Flight Center, which eased the problem. But not everyone could be moved off site: The satellite operations crew had to remain on base to be near the control center.

Teays had to house resident astronomers in a group office. These were research scientists with doctorates who each could have commanded a bookshelf-lined private office—with a window—in most academic settings. Instead, they were crammed five to a room, each with a battleship-gray desk, chair, and bookshelf, and a drawer in a file cabinet. They were rarely all present at the same time because they came in on different shifts, which reduced the sense of crowding somewhat, but it was far from ideal.

Why did it work? First, because we didn't have a choice! Second, because candidates saw the office during their hiring interviews and were fully aware of the conditions when they took the job. Third, and most important, because everyone was in the same circumstances. The more senior scientists were sharing cramped quarters with the newer ones. The on-site frontline managers were in tiny shared spaces as well. This situation precluded ego trips over who got the best office. It worked because everyone was focused on doing the job, not on their relative importance. It facilitated open communication channels, such as knowledge transfer from senior to junior personnel. It also meant that senior staff were likely to be nearby to share their experience when problems arose.

Used Is Cheaper Than New

The IUE project implemented several important technology-driven changes, with in-house staff doing much of the work. Of course, IUE's staff was very technically skilled. Their skill sets constantly evolved because these individuals were given the opportunity to develop new skills as a part of their job. They were also happy to borrow good ideas wherever they found them. There was no "not invented here" attitude. This also applied to adopting (or adapting) off-the-shelf solutions rather than always starting from scratch. Making use of trails that others have blazed optimizes your chances of success in breaking new ground even farther afield. Paying attention to the pitfalls those others encountered is a critical fault-tolerant practice.

Travel

When running lean you spend money on travel only when it is functionally necessary. For example, IUE astronomers traveled sometimes to present their research results at a professional meeting. Presenting their research results was a requirement for scientists who received grant funds, so it was functionally justified and relevant to the mission.

In addition, staff attended regular meetings with IUE's European collaborators, which meant travel to Spain or England. Remember that the bulk of IUE history occurred prior to the broad use of Internet technologies. Maintaining close collaboration among IUE's international partners required extensive discussion and working sessions on the details of operating the spacecraft and handling the data. When it makes sense for getting the work done, even the leanest operation spends the money.

Running lean requires that you send the right people to the right meetings. If a meeting is set to hammer out high-level policy issues, the big bosses need to attend. If the meeting will deal with nitty-gritty technical details, the key technical personnel need to go. Fit the participant list to the expertise needed at the meeting.

NON-IUE EXAMPLES

We have seen a lot of wasted resources going into office issues. At one organization in our post-IUE experience, the staff was constantly being moved from one office to another in an effort to ensure that precise levels of office size and amenities were preserved with each new arrival. One individual insisted—successfully—that construction plans be altered to make his office slightly larger than those of other managers because he held a position slightly higher than theirs.

Was this manager worried about luck optimization and fault tolerance in dealing with office politics? It doesn't look like it. Could he have used office configurations and assignments to build a more productive organization? Had he hired the right people he probably could have. In fact, his whole approach to office real estate probably would have been totally different had he brought a luck-optimizing approach to his role.

On another point, we have had the experience of having to manage a large number of people, including dealing with human resources issues, while housed in a cube farm, separated from everyone else by nothing but fabric half-walls. Needless to say, dealing with confidential issues was challenging. It meant time was wasted on trying to schedule meeting rooms and conducting critical phone calls when out of the office. This, we would say, is a bit too lean.

A VIRTUE OUT OF NECESSITY

IUE wasn't designed with running lean in mind; that was forced on the project by fiscal constraints. Today, everyone has to run lean just to survive in a competitive environment. In true luck-optimization fashion, you must take advantage of the benefits of running lean.

If you have hired self-renewing employees, and you have given them the opportunity and resources to learn new skills, then they are well prepared to adapt to changes in your enterprise's needs. In a collaborative work environment they will be familiar with the overall needs of the organization and you will have increased your chances of having in-house expertise available. IUE made frequent use of the staff's ever-renewing skill set. This saved the expense of hiring outside expertise when new technologies or ways of doing business developed. And, of course, it provided a lot of horsepower for the company later on, as these people moved into new positions.

In a slimmed-down workforce, everyone *must* contribute because there isn't room for anyone to coast. Your culture doesn't allow for it. A side benefit is that everyone's contribution is readily visible to the entire crew, and it is easier for you to recognize outstanding efforts.

Remember, we are not advocating that you pare down your staff to the point of inflexibility. That is not fault tolerant. You need to retain the ability to take advantage of unexpected occurrences. You need to have sufficient staff to conduct the experiments that will lead to improved ways of doing business.

Don't think in terms of malnourished drudges. Think of slender gymnasts, flexible and agile and capable of an entire repertoire of tricks.

COMMUNICATION

The CEO's role in raising a company's corporate IQ is to establish an atmosphere that promotes knowledge sharing and collaboration.

BILL GATES, CO-FOUNDER, MICROSOFT

Invariably, when someone looks at an organization and compiles a report about things that need improving, better communication is near the top of the list. Given the glut of communication tools available today, why does this continue to be such a big problem? Because the real function of communication in a business is poorly understood by most managers.

In any industry these days, knowledge is the raw material you use to make a business. Workers who handle your business's knowledge are the modern skilled laborers who rework that raw material into the solutions that make your company work better and supply the needs of your customers. And communication is what moves intermediate knowledge products through your company and delivers goods and services to your customers.

Do you need to develop luck-optimizing and fault-tolerant communication methods and procedures? You bet you do. If opportunities are not communicated to the key decision makers when they appear, leaders cannot jump on them immediately. Without good communication habits, your organization may be too slow to take advantage of a surprise opportunity and end up not getting there first. Likewise, communicating potential problems is one of the most important characteristics of a fault-tolerant organization.

COMMUNICATION CHANNELS

Designing and setting up communication channels at your organization will depend on the nature of the work, the technology used, the geographic distribution, and related factors. You will determine the exact procedures based on your specific needs, but here are some underlying luck-optimizing principles to keep in mind.

- *Communicate in all directions.* Knowledge must reach everyone. That means communication must flow in all directions—up, down, and horizontally.

- *Make communication prompt and accessible to those who need it.* Timeliness is critical, especially when communicating about organizational change. Managers and others may be in the process of making an important decision, and they can't act wisely if they don't know all the current facts.

- *Convey both good news and bad.* Everyone needs to know the truth. It's better to tell the bad news and allow everyone to commiserate together and then decide what they can do to ameliorate the situation. If you withhold the truth, you risk eroding trust.

- *Make sure the messenger of bad news is not shot.* If employees are yelled at (or worse) when they bring bad news to the boss, eventually they will avoid it. The boss will hear only happy tales and vague reports until the dragon stomps into the boardroom and incinerates everyone. This goes back to our discussion in Chapter 4 about leading a collaborative workforce. In a collaborative team, bad news is treated as a challenge that everyone needs to know about in order to solve the problem in the least time. Communication is therefore a key to the solution, not a means of assigning blame.

- *Ensure that a significant level of trust exists within the team.* If you can't trust that someone is giving you correct, complete information, you will not act boldly on the information that reaches you. You will also expend nonproductive energy on trying to verify the accuracy of the information you are receiving if trust cannot be achieved among team members.

We talked in Chapter 2 about how important it is to keep your eyes and ears attuned to what's going on in your business environment. You should not have to work hard to find out what's going on in your own organization! Tightly focused channels should be feeding you good information continuously.

You can't have a luck-optimized organization if the members don't have access to critical information. Suppose a member of your sales force learns about a hot new product that a competitor is selling, but neglects to mention it to anyone in business development or strategic planning. Can you make up market share in some other sector? If you have hired the right people and they have developed luck-optimizing work habits but you don't have effective communication, you still won't have a luck-optimized organization.

Every organization has a network of communication channels, some enterprise-wide and others more narrowly focused. A given employee will make use of any number of channels to tap into the organization's knowledge resources. When different kinds of information are separated into specific channels, employees can select just the information they need at that moment.

FOCUSED COMMUNICATION

A number of municipalities have added "non-emergency" telephone numbers to supplement their 911 services. This is because a large volume of important but not urgent calls was clogging their emergency response system and they needed to prioritize.

Your business also must set communication priorities. For example, general HR information blasted via e-mail could clog a lot of inboxes. And the tight and sensitive information used by a tiger team to respond to a twenty-four-hour response window should not leak into channels where uninvolved people can obtain it.

Suppose you want to add a new communication channel for a specific team. The channel needs to be focused exclusively on this team's activities and accessible only to its members. You will have to initiate the use of the channel in a way that sets the tone and limits the content to team needs, shepherding the process until the team has developed the habits to make best use of the channel.

Keeping communication focused and flowing through targeted channels is a vital corporate culture habit. It increases efficiency, reduces time waste and organizational confusion, and keeps people focused.

A DOCUMENTATION EXAMPLE

The shift memos from the IUE project provide an interesting example of effective communication. After every eight-hour shift, the astronomer in charge would write a brief memo summarizing the events of the shift. "No ops probs" (No operations problems) was what you wanted to read when you were coming in to take over for the next shift—but only if there really hadn't been any problems. The incoming team would read this memo first thing upon their arrival. Staff members who had been away would be able to catch up quickly when they returned by checking out the memos. In fact, everyone in operations read these memos because they contained essential information about doing their job.

The memos were quite informal. They were intended strictly for the use of the operations staff, so people felt free to speak honestly. They were also read by the frontline manager to keep apprised of events, and to ensure that the content remained focused on operations. The memo binder also held announcements and other information relevant to operations. The memos were not public, but they were archived because they contained details that might be valuable in interpreting problems with the data at a later time.

LUCK-OPTIMIZING
LESSON

Having a communication vehicle that everyone read regularly was what made the memos work. This was important because it meant that problems could be identified and solutions could be shared in an open and collegial manner.

Let's list the luck-optimizing features of this communication mechanism.

- It was informal, yet restricted to team members.

- It was part of the job description to contribute to the memos when on shift.

- It was part of the job description to read the memos daily.

- The information was nuts-and-bolts stuff about doing the job at hand.

- Any member of the work group could contribute.

- It created a simple mechanism to learn from others' mistakes and to celebrate successes.

- The frontline manager read the memos, so it was a moderated news source.

INFORMATION FROM THE TOP FLOOR

Every organization has information that comes down from top management. How often is this read by the staff? That depends largely on whether they find useful data in it. Useful—as in relevant to them, complete and reliable, timely, and honest.

Trust is something you earn slowly and can lose quickly. You need to be honest with your employees and give them accurate information. A fault-tolerant system can fall apart just as fast as trust can if faulty knowledge is acted upon.

For instance, some managers try to withhold bad news from their staff to avoid demoralizing people. But people will generally find out the bad news anyway. In a luck-optimized workplace, you and your team will take bad news in stride and treat it as a challenge. You can save a lot of time by getting your people on board quickly with new challenges. It gives you more time to turn the negative situation into a winning possibility.

There may be times when you can't talk about some development going on in the executive suite. If pressed, it is OK to simply say that you can't discuss the matter at this time. The last thing you should do is lie to your staff.

In an organization where communication is flowing as it should, people's communication needs are met. What happens when communication isn't working? Here's one example. There is a Web site that contains news about a specific government agency. The site is not, however, affiliated with the agency. Almost everyone at the agency or who works with the agency logs into this Web site regularly, if not daily. The site users also provide the journalist who runs the site with a lot of inside information. Why? We suspect that this Web site provides something the official channels do not. It frequently delivers information faster and more reliably than the official agency site. It also offers information not provided by the official site, including negative and controversial information. Such a site would not be necessary were there not a vacuum of information left by official channels.

POLICIES AND PROCEDURES

Policies and procedures are usually disseminated to employees and managers via a detailed handbook. Such a handbook tends to be an inadequate reflection of your corporate culture because most of the company's habits and traditions aren't documented there.

It is particularly important to be clear about issues that are near and dear to employees' hearts, such as raises and office assignments. A senior manager once told Teays, "We don't tell the employees about our promotion and raise process." To which Teays replied, "Too late." He had already informed his staff of the nature of the process. He was generally successful in getting his employees raises and promotions because he came prepared to support his position. How did he do this? He enlisted his staff to provide him with the necessary detailed information about their work and accomplishments, and because they understood how the process worked, they provided him with just the sort of data he needed.

INTERDEPARTMENTAL COMMUNICATION

Communication between different departments and between organizational units is frequently a problem. Why? Because it is rarely as open as it should be. It is possible to have your team working well but your progress impeded by communication breakdowns within the larger organization. *Turf battles, empire building, moats,* and *drawbridges* are some of the terms with which you will be familiar.

Some of this is inevitable once your organization reaches a certain size. Though humans are social beings, there are limits to how many people you can consider your tribe, troop, team, or what have you. It is hard to consider someone a part of your team unless you interact with them frequently. If you need to interact with someone on a daily basis, then you and that person are part of the same team, even if your official department designations are different. If you are in a larger organization, you need to think carefully about how you are communicating with other departments.

At IUE, cooperation between different departments was good, largely because individual managers focused on the success of the project and the sanctity of doing things right rather than on their own rewards and ego stroking. This meant they didn't have reason to hoard information rather than share it with other department heads. (Not that there weren't exceptions to this. The project was staffed by human beings, after all.)

THE MANAGEMENT MEETING

One of the most common interdepartmental communication vehicles is the periodic management meeting. If a meeting is going to serve as an effective communication event, then you need to think about developing effective meeting facilitation skills. Many books and training courses address this subject, and we won't dwell on it here, but here are a few pointers based on the weekly IUE managers' meeting, held with the NASA customer.

- *Keep it informal.* Don't spend time on elaborate presentation preparation. The goal is to communicate current events, successes, and challenges, not to show off your PowerPoint skills. (Teays once created a presentation for a large corporate meeting that everyone remembered for its graphics. However, no one seemed to pay any attention to the content. It was obviously not an optimal communication effort.)

- *Stick to information that affects the work of the other departments.* In other words, don't waste their time.

- *Don't assign a fixed amount of time to each department.* Sometimes a given department may not have many significant events to report, but if they have a ten-minute slot to fill, they will feel obligated to yammer on for the duration.

A final comment: The most common communication failure in otherwise good managers is that they get too busy doing what they see as the job to take time to communicate with their boss, fellow managers, and staff. Communication is an essential element of your management duties. You need to spend time on it. You need to establish a process and a habit of doing it regularly because it is an essential part of your work.

LUCK-OPTIMIZING
LESSON

Your success will depend on the support and cooperation of the other departments in your organization. To pounce on an opportunity when you see one, you have to understand enough about what is going on with other departments to know how they might support your initiative. One of the most fault-tolerant things you can do is cultivate willing allies in other departments who will help you when you are under fire.

REWARDS AND SUCCESS

Shape [your] policies so each worker will feel . . . a vital part of the company with a personal responsibility for its success and a chance to share in that success.

WILLIAM COOPER PROCTER, FORMER PRESIDENT, PROCTER & GAMBLE

Even if you hire the right people and let them do their job, you can undo the good that generates by failing to build in a system for recognizing and rewarding employees. We are not talking about rewarding people just for doing their job. That's what you pay them for. But what are you doing for people who perform beyond their job description? What are you doing for people who save you time, frustration, or the headaches that come with managing a business team?

PSYCHOLOGY OF REWARDS

It's very difficult to build rewards and other consequences into your luck-optimizing and fault-tolerant practices if your personal experience in these matters has been weak or even debilitating. The psychology of why many managers can't get a handle on the use of rewards and consequences requires deeper analysis than we can provide here. But we will suggest that if you have problems with these ideas, you are reducing your chances of success. Find a way to put your negative feelings behind you, and work with your team to develop a system of rewards and consequences that will motivate, support, and expand the types of behaviors you need to keep your business at the top of your market.

Give credit where credit is due. Praising your people for a job well done is easy, costs nothing, and works wonders. Yet it happens all too infrequently in most work environments. Why? Usually it's because the boss is too busy and distracted to take the time or remember. But sometimes it's because managers are so intent on making themselves look good that they claim exclusive credit for all the successes in their shop. (Conversely, all too often, all the blame is laid on the staff when something goes wrong.)

The International Ultraviolet Explorer project was a collaborative team environment. Project scientist Yoji Kondo went out of his way to let people know about the contributions of the staff and to compliment their expertise. The effect on morale and performance was powerful.

Many of the reports and publications of the observatory cited authorship by everyone who worked on a particular project. This made the team feel good about the work they had done, and, more important, it reinforced a desired behavior. You got recognition through team effort. You got assigned to key teams because you had contributed strongly to past team projects.

Behavior studies tell us that the positive reinforcement for a job well done must be immediate and clearly connected to the desired behavior. A manager who is too busy to say, "Good job!" to a staff member who performs well on a specific task is a manager who is too busy to focus on an especially crucial part of the job. This lack of recognition from the manager will diminish the luck-optimizing contributions of the team.

Simple acknowledgments such as posting who found the most bugs during software testing of a new product and reserving a parking space for the "employee of the month" may seem trivial, but praise works best when it is public for many reasons:

- The value of being praised is enhanced for the recipient.

- The other employees see that praise is the result of outstanding performance.

- The staff learns that this is the culture of your team.

- Upper management gets a better view of the quality of your team.

- Everyone's morale gets a notable boost.

REWARDS AND JOB SATISFACTION

Job satisfaction is perhaps the most underappreciated and least understood aspect of the system of rewards and consequences. Yet it relates to everything from performance to retention. If it is possible to create job satisfaction in a given business, it is advantageous to all.

IUE experience clearly indicates that physical conditions are not the key to job satisfaction. Far from it. As an increasingly aging project, we tended to get shunted off into older spaces with increasingly obsolete equipment. Refurbishments were rare, and we have already mentioned every single one that happened during the project's almost nineteen years. And yet job satisfaction was high. As a result, we had a community of people who could be trusted to do their best every day. We had open communication, which helped us create solutions quickly. Everyone was willing to help when asked. We were all in it together, and we all worked it out together as well.

TYPES OF REWARDS

Let's look at some of the rewards commonly used in a business setting.

Bonuses and Rewards

Everyone appreciates money. It's a pretty clear indication that the organization values your work. Large cash bonuses and lavish awards will

LUCK-OPTIMIZING LESSON

Your hiring process should place people in positions in which they achieve high levels of job satisfaction. People who like and feel good about what they do, and who have pride in the skill it takes to do their job, are rewarded every day they show up. They can express themselves effectively through their work. They are paid well enough that they are comfortable at home. They perceive that they are trusted by management, and they behave accordingly.

affect the bottom line, however. In many cases, smaller, more frequent, and more widely distributed awards will have a greater return on investment. Teays was once questioned by someone from upper management about his giving out $100 awards: "Won't the employee be insulted by such a small amount?" Maybe in the executive suite, but not out in the trenches! If you have selected the right people and are letting them do their job, you are likely to have many people who deserve some recognition for efforts above and beyond their job description. By rewarding their behavior you increase the chances that they will continue to perform at peak levels.

Teays regularly takes his staff out to lunch. He began this practice while at IUE and has found it to be an effective management tool in subsequent positions. It allows him to thank the team for their outstanding performance, as a team. Being out of the office also has an important psychological effect: Everyone is more relaxed and feels more comfortable talking about things that might not otherwise come up.

Raises

Salaries and raises are always a concern for employees, so your chances of success as a manager are optimized if you attend carefully to how you go about determining them. In many organizations the pay increase allowed in the annual raise process is rather limited and does not sufficiently reflect differences in performance of individuals. In a situation like this, you may have to pay more attention to less traditional methods of recognition, such as those we've discussed in preceding paragraphs.

IUE had a great deal of success hiring freshouts, people just graduating (with bachelor's, master's, or doctoral degrees). The starting pay was not especially high, but because there was a noticeable difference in percentage increases for the highest-performing employees, everyone could see a real benefit to outstanding efforts.

One of the quickest ways to minimize your luck is to set up a system that provides the same level of raise to everyone, regardless of how well they performed. While many businesses have introduced bonus and other merit pay programs, salaries are still most commonly based on seniority rather than performance. If you follow this practice, you are actively training your staff to put in minimum effort, since that still gets the maximum reward.

Another approach to discouraging productive behavior has surfaced recently. If your staff sees the CEO getting a huge raise while the company struggles, it will be difficult to convince them that compensation is based on performance.

The Right Yardstick

A minor note, but a revealing one: Many organizations consider it unacceptable to have employees making more money than their immediate supervisor. However, in the modern information technology world, a technical specialist with long experience may be more valuable to the organization than the unit manager and may require higher compensation to keep on staff. Your job is to ensure that each of your valuable workers has the resources and opportunity to use his or her experience and expertise to produce for the organization. Worrying about relative pay scales does nothing to help optimize either your luck or that of the organization.

LUCK-OPTIMIZING
LESSON

The following questions are important for techies considering moving to management:

- At the end of the day, if your team has produced a significant accomplishment in which you did not play an active role, will you feel pride and satisfaction in your team's success?

- Do you have to contribute hands-on effort in the solution to feel that you have accomplished something?

- If you want your team to come up with innovations for you, can you let go sufficiently to let them do it?

Offices with a View

The whole business of how you identify the right people to promote to management parallels the ideas we discussed in Chapter 5 for hiring the right people in the first place. We all have heard that people should be promoted based on their ability, but how do you identify those with management ability? Charlie Wu told us that in the early days of IUE, "[We would] keep our eyes open to see who has the leadership potential." This worked fine in a small start-up, but in a larger organization you will probably need a more systematic approach to optimize your luck in identifying potential new managers. Chapter 6, on delegation, indicates how you can assess management potential in your staff. By delegating tasks to people, including tasks that involve leading a team, you can see whether they have the aptitude for management. Employees also find out whether they enjoy management tasks.

A common problem when moving technical people into management positions is the new managers' desire to continue to do the technical work they love, rather than concentrating on their new management tasks. Sometimes this can be resolved by making someone serve as the

Alpha Geek (OK, the Chief Technical Officer, or some such title) and having someone else fulfill the manager role.

Track Flexibility

Having various career tracks, including technical and management tracks, is one important practice a number of larger corporations use. If the tracks are well designed, technical people can continue to increase their income, perks, reporting level, and other opportunities in sync with an equivalent managerial track. The important factor is that they don't have to become managers to improve their salary and general environment, but can continue doing technical work at senior levels. It should also be easy to jump back and forth between managerial and technical tracks. If switching tracks is common, based on the needs of the organization or its customers, it will be easier for people to try out a management track—and revert to a technical track if it turns out that management isn't for them. In other words, you are building in fault tolerance to the job assignment process—the ability to conduct an experiment and correct something that isn't working.

CSC made use of this process and both Teays and Meylan switched back and forth between management and technical tracks as needed. In a smaller organization you may not have a formal track structure, but the essential concept is still usable.

The bottom line is that recognition through promotion requires more than one definition. Alternatives for career advancement and pay raises should exist that don't require all employees to follow a single track. From the employees' perspective, this means they won't have to pursue a management position because it's the only road to higher pay. If they pursue management, it will be because they have the desire and the potential to succeed at it.

REWARDS AS TRAINING

When most people talk about rewards in the workplace they are talking about the effect of rewards on employee morale and how this improves productivity. Yes, this is important. Remember, however, that your rewards system effectively trains your team to act in specific ways. Set up your system of rewards to produce and reinforce luck-optimizing behaviors. A rewards system that is consistent with your organization's goals is one of the surest methods for informal training of staff in your corporate culture.

CONSEQUENCES OF POOR PERFORMANCE

We have been talking about how to align your rewards system to optimize your chances of encouraging good performance. But what if you have a poorly performing employee? What happens when you have created a rewards system to encourage people, and they still don't perform? If you've hired carefully, the chances of this happening are minimized, but it still can happen. What if an employee who once performed well has fallen off in performance? Or, the most common problem, what if you inherited employees who aren't producing the way you would like?

Dealing with underperforming employees is one of the least pleasant tasks you perform as a manager. We've always said that management is hard work; not just hard in the sense that you have to be industrious, but also in that you have to be tough at times.

If you have to intervene to correct an employee's performance or behavior, there are some important things to remember. Remember that, like rewards, criticisms should be immediate and closely connected to the behavior to provide maximum reinforcement. Remember also that, while making praise public enhances its value, criticism should be delivered as privately as possible.

Perhaps the most important thing to remember when discussing poor performance with an employee is to remain calm and factual. Be concrete about what behavior or output is unacceptable and how it affects the team's ability to get the job done. Be clear about your expectations for future performance.

Ultimately, you may have to let an employee go. It is never pleasant, and it is usually a slow and painstaking process. This is the very reason we urged you, in Chapter 5, to spend so much careful effort on hiring.

Since the firing process is so painful, the natural inclination is to avoid it as long as possible. This is the avoidance of discomfort that is at the root of drive satisfaction, as we discussed in Chapter 4. But the long-range, luck-optimizing view allows you to realize that a bit of discomfort now will save you much greater pain in the long run. You must also consider the effect on your other employees of allowing an employee to continue to underperform. Taking care of the problem when it is small is the most fault-tolerant approach.

The point we are making about how you optimize your luck through your reward system for your employees is simply this: Your method of rewarding employees should encourage the behavior you want your employees to show. If your system of rewards isn't accomplishing this, then your chances of getting and sustaining outstanding performance from your people are very small.

If your system of rewards is designed well, it will optimize your luck by helping you retain the best employees and providing encouragement for them to continue to overdeliver on a daily basis.

THE CULTURE

PART THREE

THEORY OF THE
LUCK-OPTIMIZING CULTURE

Corporate culture is everything.
JEFFREY R. IMMELT, CHAIRMAN AND CEO, GENERAL ELECTRIC

When we began interviewing IUE managers for this book, we wanted to find out how the project's culture got started and how it became an incubator of innovation and customer satisfaction. Why was this important to us? Because after we worked at the project, we worked at places where the culture was unfocused, where luck optimization and fault tolerance were not practiced in any meaningful sense. What were people in these places doing instead? In some cases they were competing to build their career instead of collaborating to build a strong business. In other cases they were preserving their context so effectively that they could convince top management that change was impossibile. Based on our discussion of drive satisfaction strategies with respect to leadership (in Chapter 4), this should come as no surprise. The surprise is that we worked at a place where a good counterexample existed: the collaborative culture at IUE.

Throughout this book we've compared IUE's practices with those of some places we worked after leaving the project. Now it's time to move from the level of practices to the level of culture.

UNDERSTANDING THE BUSINESS IMPACTS OF A LUCK-OPTIMIZING CULTURE

After years of discussion, we concluded that the evolution of a luck-optimizing culture is affected by five closely related elements (illustrated in Figure 2). Let's start by defining these elements and then examine each more thoroughly.

- *Values.* The reasons you get the corporate culture you get
- *Corporate culture.* The behavioral habits through which your company conducts its business
- *Organizational idealism or cynicism.* The emotional result of the degree to which the corporate culture facilitates employees' sense of personal success, or fails to do so
- *Product.* The marketable result of corporate culture
- *Marketplace acceptance or rejection.* The positive or negative response of the market to your product, and to your company as a result of that product

Values

The founding IUE managers never really talked about values. They emphasized observation and response. Their actions, however, demonstrated that customer satisfaction was their highest value. They worked hard to please NASA, and they worked hard to please their guest observers.

We've defined *values* as the reasons you get the corporate culture you do. That means that your organization's habits form around the values the leadership holds. This distinguishes values as they usually operate in an organization from what may be called "lofty ideals."

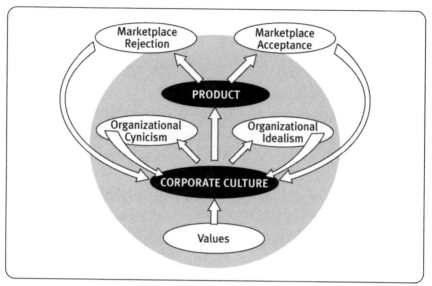

FIGURE 2 ▸ FLOW OF THE FIVE ELEMENTS INFLUENCING
A LUCK-OPTIMIZING CULTURE

Experience suggests that people intuitively understand this distinction. A "Statement of Values" posted for public view is usually judged on the basis of what the company actually does. If employees aren't treated according to the values posted on the wall, they often develop a cynical attitude about such statements. On the other hand, if everyone is operating strictly on the basis of self-interested values without regard to the success of the organization, then the habits of the culture attain little focus for achieving the big business goals.

Are values important? Of course; they are vital. Just look at the IUE example. IUE formed its habits around customer satisfaction, and the customers told us they were happy with us. Now look at the Enron example. What have the judges and the juries said about the habits there? What would we conclude about the values driving those habits?

Commonly held values at IUE included customer satisfaction, operational efficiency, and the ability to innovate to accomplish those two things. There was a love for astronomy, and there was pride associated with being part of the U.S. space program. There was personal pride in a job well done. And, to IUE people, a job well done meant that they did it better than they did it the last time.

People, and businesses, behave on the basis of their values. The best way to understand their values is to watch them behave.

Corporate Culture

This book has presented a "systems approach" to building success as a leader or manager. This means you want to set up methods and procedures that help people repeat their on-the-job successes as often as possible. As your top-level business system, your corporate culture should be set up to capture methods and procedures that have demonstrated usefulness in helping people reprise successful business behaviors. Corporate culture should also contain habits of innovation for all aspects of your business. While innovation is often thought of as what you do to create a new product or service for the market, it is also vital for improving the way your business operates. Cultural habits of innovation solve issues involving change management, too.

As shown in Figure 2, corporate culture is where production occurs within the organization. The product of your culture has to pass the test of market acceptance, and you have to be able to respond to acceptance or rejection in luck-optimizing and fault-tolerant ways. Values have some input to corporate culture, but the guidance that values can provide is limited to the consistency with which they are followed by the leadership and the workers.

The goal in engineering a luck-optimizing culture is to create habits for your workers that make it easier for them to do their job and to deliver a product that satisfies the market. The more they can rely on good habits that generate a sought-after product, including habits of change as needed, the more often they will succeed in satisfying the market.

Organizational Idealism or Cynicism

Figure 2 also shows two feedback loops that will either reinforce and strengthen a successful corporate culture or erode and weaken a sub-

LUCK-OPTIMIZING LESSON

These factors defined organizational idealism at the International Ultraviolet Explorer project:

- The managers and staff all took great pride in their work.
- They took great pride in the IUE "brand."
- They perceived change as an opportunity to improve IUE's standing with customers.

standard one. The first loop delivers the feedback workers send out into the culture's habits. This feedback registers their ability to satisfy their personal measures of success while working for a company. If they feel their work is a positive part of their life, they are likely to contribute to improvements in the company, even if only in a small way. In this case, the culture is generating *organizational idealism* in the workforce. Conversely, if workers feel their work experience is a drain on their life, they are more likely to contribute to the inability of the company to deliver a product to the market that could satisfy a customer. This culture is generating *organizational cynicism.*

Organizational idealism will ordinarily motivate people to link their good work habits with the good habits already in place within the culture. At IUE this was a vital part of remaining innovative and positive in the face of extreme technical or political difficulties. After these many years since the project ended, the idea of organizational idealism remains one of the most talked-about features of our work experience when we get together.

Unfortunately, organizational cynicism has been a common part of our work experience, and the experience of many of our peers and reports, since leaving IUE. It was the contrast between the organizational

LUCK-OPTIMIZING LESSON

Here are some conditions that define organizational cynicism that IUE workers have encountered since the project ended.

- Line workers experience a caste system that upper management doesn't even perceive.
- An army of consultants eats up resources and operates in an unprofessional manner, creating anger, frustration, and perhaps a sense of futility among in-house employees.
- Promises are made but not kept.
- A sense exists that it doesn't matter how well you perform because somebody who "sucks up" better than you are willing to will advance more quickly.

idealism we experienced at IUE and the organizational cynicism we encountered in other workplaces that motivated us to write this book. Before our research into this difference we thought, as most do, that this emotional response *was* the culture. We asked, "Why do some organizations excel at achieving their business objectives and leave employees with smiles on their faces, while other organizations don't?" Now we understand this emotional response to be the result of corporate culture, and not the culture itself. If habits within the corporate culture help people succeed by their own standards, they will be happy. If habits within the culture make doing the job harder, they won't.

Product

Your corporate culture creates what you sell—that is, your product (see Figure 2). You could sell cars. You could sell accounting. You could sell energy. At IUE we sold the ability to do world-class science. Our business processes were designed to help us get more data for each guest observer. They were revamped to get data to guest observers more quickly. Our business processes included the constant improvement of data quality and ease of analysis. Our customers were also part of our business process evolution, advising us from the years before launch through mission shutdown on what they would like and how we might get it for them.

When looked at a certain way, the corporate culture of the IUE project functioned just like factory equipment. But, instead of using machines to make jelly and fill jars, it used the minds of its people to create products for sale. Instead of using an assembly line to build cars, it used people connected to good communication systems to move complex services to readiness for customer consumption.

Any group in a company whose people squabble instead of collaborate is like a machine that drops full jars of jelly onto the concrete factory floor. That means the corporate culture is out of adjustment just like the jelly jar machine. If you have people who gum up communication channels with nonbusiness chatter, that's like an assembly line that has to be shut down until it can be reconfigured for production. That means the business processes in your corporate culture are full of potential production failures just like that assembly line.

For any business, the corporate culture really is functionally the same as equipment on a factory floor. And just like factory equipment, that corporate culture can be engineered, adjusted, tweaked, and tuned up—or left unmaintained, ungreased, unadjusted, and even unpowered.

That's how important corporate culture is to a business. Any behavior that doesn't contribute to business success is like a machine that breaks good product before it gets off the line. Any habits that slow down your ability to deliver something to sell are parts of your culture that require reengineering.

Marketplace Acceptance or Rejection

The second feedback loop shown in Figure 2 tells you how well your corporate culture is doing in terms of market response to your product. Do people use it? Do they like it? Is it the only choice they have? There used to be a lot of resentment toward Microsoft because there were no other commonly available choices, but people still bought it because "that's what everyone else has."

In many respects, the IUE project created a new product in astronomy: the ability to study objects in space that shine with ultraviolet (UV) light. Earth's atmosphere blocks out UV light, so unless you have rockets and satellites to get you above the air, you can't see the UV light coming from stars and galaxies. For many years the project monopolized the market for its product. However, the project didn't take this monopoly for granted. Everyone knew that the Hubble Space Telescope was coming, so they said, "We'd better do this job well to stay in the game when it goes up."

And that's the way things worked. Most astronomers were used to how things operated in ground-based astronomy, in those big mountaintop domes . So the IUE project set up its services to operate the same way. Everything was nice and familiar. And those parts of the operation that were beyond the abilities of the guest observers, like running a satellite, were simply taken care of for them. Guest observers only had to tell the operations people what they wanted, and, within the limits of what the satellite could do, the IUE staff got it for them.

The service orientation of the IUE staff is still considered by many to be the best ever in the astronomical community. That feedback from the community, the market's acceptance of IUE services, reinforced the behaviors the staff practiced. We were doing a good job, we were told we were doing a good job, and we strove to do things better each time we had a task.

In a corporate culture that is helping people repeat their successes, positive feedback from the market is a good boost, and it encourages people to continue in their customer-delighting practices. In a good culture, negative feedback is taken seriously because, as a team with organizational idealism (perhaps here call it "pride"), the workers want to eliminate negative feedback. Negative feedback in a good culture does not lead to a breakdown in work ethic, or productivity, or things like that. It leads to changes in habits to get back onto a customer-delighting track. So feedback on marketplace rejection will still usually get a positive reaction from the workers in a good, strong, enabling culture.

Negative market response is bad news to a weak or unfocused culture. In a weak culture, one that disables repeatable success, bad news from the market will lead to further business-disabling behavior. In an unfocused culture people might want to try to fix things, but they often won't know what to do or how to begin.

Ultimately, if your corporate culture cannot deliver product that the market accepts, you will go out of business. This is why your corporate culture must be engineered to facilitate the success of everyone in your company. Everyone in your organization must be able to repeat successful business behaviors as quickly and easily as possible. If your workers are in situations where change is a daily reality, then their habits need to revolve around careful observation of change and innovation to respond effectively to it.

THOUGHTS ON INTEGRITY

We haven't talked about integrity in the corporate culture because IUE leadership didn't talk about it. Here's an illustration of the reasoning.

> South Korea's top university issued a public apology today after an investigative panel ruled that disgraced professor Hwang Woo-suk faked all of his human stem cell research. Seoul National University president Chung Un-chan called Hwang's fraud "an unwashable blemish on the whole scientific community as well as our country" and a "criminal act in academia." (*Boston Globe,* January 11, 2006)

How did Hwang Woo-suk get caught? Simple. Other geneticists read his papers and attempted to replicate his results. When it became clear that his methods didn't work anywhere else in the world, people probed deeper until it became clear that he had lied.

In any of the physical science communities (including astrophysics where IUE belonged), no assertion is allowed to slide. Everybody's work is checked to see if it holds up. The scientific communities demand and enforce accountability from practicing scientists.

In the business community, it would be like making all your accounting systems open for audit, at any time, by any interested party, especially the competition and the IRS.

Integrity was the habit at IUE, both in terms of science delivered and in terms of dealing with customers, because, as scientists, the people who worked at IUE really didn't know how to act any differently. Integrity is a critical cultural element that optimizes success in scientific communities.

We don't believe that integrity is unique to the scientific community. Whether in science or in business, the practice of integrity is a choice based on payoff. Science doesn't work without it. No good business can either.

FINAL THOUGHT ON CULTURE THEORY

In this model we've repeatedly emphasized repeatable results. We've asserted that cultures that help people succeed in their jobs are the corporate culture engineer's goal. That being said, adaptability is perhaps the most important repeatable behavior in modern business. People need systems that help them make changes and transitions. The corporate culture needs those capabilities built into it as well. When you think through the process to create repeatable behaviors of success, include the repeatable ability to change and adapt in preparation for new ways to succeed when the marketplace demands them.

LUCK-OPTIMIZING LESSON

Here are some basic habits to follow that can lead to consistently ethical behavior:

- If you focus on your enterprise's success to the exclusion of personal gain, and you hire people who do the same, integrity is likely to become a cultural habit in your business.

- Truthful communication about failures and problems has to be valued just as highly as the communication of successes.

- The breadth of collaborative behavior in an organization serves as a gauge for integrity, since collaboration requires integrity to achieve the greatest gain.

12

CREATION OF THE LUCK-OPTIMIZING CULTURE

I felt the only way to turn things around was to get people to think like owners.

JACK STACK, CEO, SRC HOLDING

The example of the International Ultraviolet Explorer project suggests that the person functioning as leader is the person actively engineering the characteristics of the organization's culture. That's how you would distinguish a leader from an alpha climber, for instance. But, the founding IUE managers weren't consciously thinking, "Boy, I want a luck-optimizing, fault-tolerant culture that helps people succeed every day." They were simply dedicated to working hard to please their customers, and they added likeminded people to their teams.

Yet this simple description of their leadership behaviors suggests that cultures are engineered at two levels: First, the leader acquires the range of skills and perspectives needed to succeed personally. Second, the rest of the team emulates many of these same skills and perspectives. In the spirit of "leading by example," the leader's skills for success need to be visible enough for people to understand and follow. When you add systematic training in success-building skills, you are likely to have engineered an empowering corporate culture.

This chapter attempts to do a couple of things. It provides a recap or review of the book's chapters and main points. And, where applicable, it points out the skills that you need to push down into your workforce. If it's important for you to be a good communicator, for example, it's probably important for everybody in your group to be a good communicator.

If this chapter seems somewhat long on What and short on How, remember that we believe in delegation. That's where leaders specify What and the delegates figure out How. There's a practical reason for this, too. Suppose 100,000 people read this book. There's no way we could include Hows for 100,000 different skill sets or map those skill sets to 100,000 different business contexts. The recipe that might work for one reader isn't likely to work for the other 99,999.

Remember, too, that recipes are not luck optimizing and fault tolerant. A recipe is a one-problem solution. We want you to learn how to solve problems in the general sense, and to be able to teach your teams how to solve problems as well. The Whats we've supplied are the targets you try to hit. You keep running experiments until you do.

RELATIONSHIP MANAGEMENT

Every aspect of your business is driven by relationships. This isn't merely a matter of getting along; over time you will have conflicts with trusted people in your company, with your suppliers, and with your customers. When that happens, you want the fault-tolerant features of your culture to turn the problems into luck-optimizing relationship opportunities.

- *Good communication.* Relationships work best when all parties are clear about the issues and purposes that bring them together. Clarity is achieved through frequent, to-the-point communication and by asking for feedback on what is understood. If you want to make sure people know what's going on, ask them to tell you what's going on.

- *Respect.* Respect drives many behaviors in relationships. Chief among these is keeping promises and agreements. Next is the flexibility of the relationship to renegotiate promises and agreements if necessary. These behaviors reveal options that build luck optimization and fault tolerance in relationships. A trusted ally who spots an opportunity that could be mutually beneficial will more likely share it with you. And if a difficulty with an agreement crops up between allies, years of respect and trust generate the fault tolerance that keeps the relationship together for future opportunity.

Practice good habits of communication in everything you do. Strive to be clear in what you say and to understand what other parties say.

Make it a habit to keep your promises and agreements and, if you can't, make it a habit to reopen negotiations as soon as you know you need to. Don't let a problem fester. Most people in your network would rather not have you fail because that creates another whole set of problems for them!

These will become cultural-level habits when everyone in your organization does the same. Train your personnel in good communication practices. It's a major investment with great returns. Also, train your people in the simple ethics of keeping promises and agreements.

Cultural habits can generate clear communication and fulfilled promises, or they can generate muddy communication and broken promises—and there's a big difference in the business performance that results from one or the other. People who develop luck-optimizing communication habits build stronger long-term relationships, and more of them, than those who don't.

 Experience strongly suggests that people are no longer trained to keep their word. At IUE, in contrast, staff members were trained not to hedge their language. We knew the capabilities we had and the services we could deliver. If a guest observer wanted to try something new we could promise to study the feasibility. We didn't promise to do anything more until the feasibility was verified.

CONTINUOUS OBSERVATION

Observation is the first source of knowledge. What are the practical ways you can observe, and what cultural-level habits of observation do you want to perform?

- *Watch your direct customers.* In your travels to customer sites, watch the people, pay attention to the physical surroundings, and make note of how they use language. Bring people with you who will do the same. You may need to pay particular attention to the person heading your meeting, so let the people with you take special note of the other things they're good at picking up.

- *Keep up with the news.* Whether national news or the news of your industry, subscribe and read. Search the Web and capture innovations of interest to your business.

- *Use information consumers.* There are likely to be people in your organization who are always scrounging up interesting information. Get them targeted on some of your informational needs, teach them how to sift for what you want, and let them do some observing for you.

- *Train for a culture of observation.* Reward everyone who brings you usable observations. What do they see in the market? What do they hear from the competition? What do they hear from co-workers that you need to act on? You need this information, so generate a system of rewards that will produce it.

WORKING HARD

On the assumption that your example will be followed by your employees, what do you want "working hard" to mean in terms of corporate habits? Here are some habits from IUE:

- Getting at things now
- Working until things are finished

- Devoting time to finding ways to work smarter

- Working hard to ensure customer satisfaction

- Working hard to help each other succeed

Is there room in this for rest or celebration of a job well done? Certainly. Rest and celebration are much more satisfying when they are earned. And it's important that people feel good about what they are doing.

Working hard isn't always fun, but if the assignments are clear and make sense, hard work is acceptable. If there are crunch times or tasks of peculiar difficulty to complete, increase incentives to increase motivation. And keep your promises to pay off when the job gets done.

CRITICAL THINKING

Good hard thinking is where the best companies make their money. Critical thinking is based in asking questions and analyzing currently known facts. Obviously, the observations you collect are a vital part of critical thinking. You ask questions about the information you and your organization have collected, and you analyze these data for clues about how to approach current business situations. At the cultural level, you need to train your people in some simple critical thinking skills. Again, some hints from IUE:

- What has changed (about anything) since we last looked at . . . ?

- What do these changes tell us about our current business context?

- What opportunities do we need to start gearing up for based on these changes?

- What parts of our business do we need to reinforce with various fault-tolerant protections?

- What can we do to improve current business processes?

- What painful things might we need to face if we are going to succeed?

Critical thinking takes nothing for granted. Past successes can be repeated, but it's better to improve upon them than to accept them as the standard for your business's performance in the future. The fundamental question for the critically thinking culture is

- What can we do to improve . . . (service, products, or anything else about our company)?

LUCK-OPTIMIZING TEAM MEMBERS

Enterprise-wide habits must be designed intentionally to generate a culture that helps people replicate success. This includes hiring methods and procedures. For instance, everyone who hires should look for people who can think independently. Independent thinkers also need to be able to work effectively in a team setting. Your hiring methods and procedures should be built to discover those people in the review process.

You want your hiring methods and procedures to generate repeatable results for everyone who will use them. You don't develop methods and procedures for the purpose of creating a uniform process. This isn't a means of generating a one-size-fits-all approach to hiring, which isn't likely to be luck-optimizing. Instead, you develop methods and procedures that help people succeed.

Loosely speaking, your hiring practices should embody processes that screen applicants for:

- Emotional fit
- Work ethic
- Independent thinking
- Collaborative habits
- Luck-optimizing and fault-tolerant approaches to personal success
- Needed skills

We outlined the IUE process for identifying hires that fit into the project in Chapter 5. There are other approaches available. Some people use psychological assessments to screen applicants. Some use "behavioral interviewing" to great success. There is also the cookbook approach provided by the book *Topgrading,* by B. D. Smart (Penguin, 2005). Cookbook approaches are useful as long as you make sure the primary characteristics of your organization are accounted for when you use them.

When it comes to maximizing luck optimization and fault tolerance, you may want a whole bunch of help. If you hire only to fill a position, you're limiting your ability to build a powerful team. Keep the corporate culture you want in mind when you make your hires, and make sure all your other managers do the same.

DELEGATION

Frequently throughout this book we've linked the ability to delegate with confidence to good hiring. If you've hired people whose workplace values strongly resemble yours, then your organization should be able to construct a focused corporate culture. This gives your business a great potential advantage in the market; if your competition does not have an equally focused culture, it may be unable to compete against you effectively.

A cultural habit of delegation should also promote habits of cooperation. This is particularly important when creativity and innovation are required to respond to change or to break through long-standing barriers to corporate progress. In an environment full of intelligent, creative people, the range of expertise will often require flexibility within the group when it comes to leadership on specific topics: When the topic calls for it, the group's authority on a specific topic might temporarily direct the activities of the group to optimize their ability to succeed. In such cases, even leadership becomes a delegated activity.

We also noted that delegation is not an emotionally natural undertaking. But, an ability to solve problems recognizes delegation as a solution to many problems. To overcome emotional conflict with delegation we have to extend trust in our first delegated assignment to someone. If that person earns our trust by fulfilling our expectations, our emotional barrier to delegation weakens.

Delegation is, of course, a personal practice. We choose whom we trust to carry out what we need done. But, as a cultural habit, the entire organization needs to learn something of the give and take when requests are made among group members and the promises to fulfill requests are kept.

Delegation also generates organizational idealism. It is interpersonal teaming at a one-to-one level. It implies trust, trustworthiness, mentoring, and a commitment to each person's success. When leaders commit to delegate effectively, the effects reverberate throughout the organization.

ADAPTABILITY

In Chapter 7 we discussed the tension between habits of success and the need to change when the environment demands it. We concluded that a corporate culture needs to include methods and procedures to create new habits when either opportunity or challenge appears in your business context.

The big motivators for change are avoidance of discomfort and better payoff for efforts expended. These two motivators stimulate both our emotions (such as fear and satisfaction) and our interest and abilities in creating solutions.

Anecdotal evidence suggests that most changes in an organization affect people negatively: They'll need to give up time with their family because of the change. They'll be working more hours with no more pay. They'll be working fewer hours with less pay. Anecdotal evidence also suggests that corporate cultures can turn a change into a bad habit. In these companies, people have to change, and it's always painful. There is no way to avoid pain or enhance payoff. (This is also a likely sign of a poorly run business.)

We've continually asserted that change is always happening and that luck optimization and fault tolerance is the most effective approach to change. Adaptability as a cultural habit is perhaps the engine that makes this work for everyone in your organization. But, if the only way you deal with change is by moving pain from the bottom line to the line workers, you need to improve your use of adaptability now. How do you go about that?

- Contrary to popular belief, business problems are relationship problems, not money problems. Somewhere in your network of suppliers, employees, or customers you have a relationship problem to solve. Be brave. Ask the people involved what they like about their relationship with you, and what they don't like. Design a self-training program (like IUE people would) to build on specific relationship strengths and fix specific weaknesses based on what you hear. If you don't know how to build a self-training program, get training or coaching or whatever it takes to learn how to fix relationships and get them to work for you.

- The inability to manage change is often based on a lack of observation. Something big sneaks up on you; so big that people wonder how you missed it; so big that they actually have been telling you about it for months. Be observant. Listen to those around you.

- Engage your luck-optimizing culture. If you don't have one, start working on one. Then, when you observe a change, pull the people you need together to design the best response.

Now that gives you some starting points for dealing with change on a leadership level. Let's assume that you've designed a positive business response to a major change. How does that flow through your organization, and how will you help your people make changes that help you and help them as well?

- *Relationship management.* In the first half of the twentieth century the big manufacturing companies had adversarial relationships with their employees. Many such companies retain an adversarial attitude. Others treat their employees like children who can't be trusted and so withhold information from them. Hiring to produce a luck-optimizing culture means that you bring people on who can handle the truth about the business and what it faces in the market. They feel comfortable sharing their observations, and you share your observations and propose responses. If you include your people in the formation of those responses, they will be prepared for needed changes.

- *Communication.* Managing relationships effectively implies a lot of communication between leadership and employees: Everyone is aware of the changes going on in the marketplace, and, increasingly, everyone has a part in formulating responses to them.

If good relationship management and communication are corporate habits, everyone will be prepared to adapt when the time comes. Everyone will be able to see change coming. And, everyone will work to adjust their behaviors.

A LEAN OPERATION

If you have too many people in your organization, some of them are going to end up with too much time on their hands. This means that they will have time to behave in a way that de-focuses the habits of your corporate culture. Now, you may say, "Having a few extra bodies around is our fault-tolerant position in case of trouble. If there's an opportunity that calls for more talent, it's there ready to go."

Wrong. An overstaffed organization contains more faults than it defends against, by about as many as you have extra bodies. Idle people take up space, cost money to maintain, and pose a potential hazard to other parts of the organization.

Idle people are noticed by, and create frustration for, busy people. This affects performance due to increasing organizational cynicism, and eventually your busy people will become like your idle people. That's basic human nature. Why set yourself up for that kind of trouble? Keep things lean.

The upside is that people in a slightly understaffed situation, such as we had at IUE, will feel the importance of their job on a daily basis. This means that they will experience organizational idealism, which motivates them to perform to the best of their abilities each day. Performing to the best of your abilities each day is a powerful cultural habit.

COMMUNICATION

It is important to take the time to train your organization in basic communication skills. Simplicity and directness are perhaps the two most important luck-optimizing and fault-tolerant habits in clear communication. If you require complicated sentences and big words to be clear, that's fine. Scientists use them all the time to great effect. But if a scientist can get a point across with five words that add up to six syllables in one sentence, that is exactly what the good ones will do. For optimal clarity, it's best to get to the point as directly as possible.

When it comes to ego, status, and other issues of self-perception, good communication frequently loses. We all identify deeply with just about everything we say. In a healthy, luck-optimizing culture, clarity makes a person stand out in the best of ways, while verbal posturing and self-stroking make a person stand out in negative ways. Clarity always works in a culture striving for luck optimization and fault tolerance.

REWARDS AND REINFORCEMENT FOR LUCK OPTIMIZATION AND FAULT TOLERANCE

You, as the big boss, might be able to define and distribute big cash rewards for certain kinds of performance. If people have earned them, distribute them. This is a big part of relationship management—giving back when it's time to give back.

Other organization-wide habits of reward are also important. Some of these habits are as simple as social greases (or, perhaps, social graces) where gratitude is always expressed for help received. This should operate at every level; even nonmanagerial people should acknowledge the helpful behaviors of others in the everyday routine. Do you want helpful behavior pervading your company? Get everyone to say, "Thank you" when they get good help from their co-workers.

In a work environment like the IUE project, where we were under-funded to the point that we were always running a worker or two short, there weren't large amounts of money set aside for out-of-cycle bonuses or other rewards. Here are some of the practices we used to make sure people got the recognition they deserved.

- We made sure that the people who did the work got full credit for the work.
  - They made their own presentations in meetings with customers.
  - Their special efforts and accomplishments were reported to the NASA customer in weekly meetings.
  - They published under their own names in official IUE technical releases for use by guest observers.
- We frequently took an employee out to lunch to thank him or her for a specific piece of work.
- We occasionally took our sections out to lunch to thank the team for a period of special performance.
- We applied for cash bonuses (usually small) from CSC for outstanding performers.

These were not periodic or systematic rewards. They were rewards that appeared as the situation called for them. We believe that this expanded the experience of organizational idealism among IUE people. We weren't merely being nice. We were also managing our relationships to reinforce the luck-optimizing and fault-tolerant behaviors that they so often produced for us.

LEADERSHIP

The roots of leadership are in face-to-face task-oriented situations. Leadership started out as a transient social feature that occasionally appeared when a group needed special solutions. When the problem went away, so did the behaviors of leadership.

This model of transient leadership is powerful as a cultural habit. In an adaptable corporate culture, you are usually free to pick the most capable person to lead a specific, temporary, task. You also, then, aren't saddled with a permanent assignment. The next time a task-oriented group is needed, the best person to lead *that* group can be assigned to move things to success.

We did this all the time at IUE. Teays assigned his top technical resident astronomer to manage his major operations refurbishment. Meylan empowered his senior technical lead to pursue funding to convert the ultraviolet astronomy data from all earlier NASA missions into a standardized format that all astronomers could use. The technical lead obtained grants and led the project. When these jobs were finished, these leadership roles went away.

If you have hired well, you'll almost always have good-caliber temporary leaders wherever you need them. Your culture, however, needs to have habits that allow these leaders to come forward. Here are some starting ideas to help you make that happen.

- Identify the person with the passion for the job that needs to be done—not the person with the passion to become a manager.

- Does this person have the requisite expertise to lead the team? This person doesn't need to have all the technical expertise to do the work but will need to be respected by the team that will perform the task.

- Can this person articulate a reasonable starting approach? The initial plan may not work. However, by looking through the proposed plan, you can gain a sense of how the potential leader for this task is thinking about getting to the goal. If he or she can puzzle out a few Plan B alternatives as well, your selection of this person to lead the task is likely to be sound.

Remember that leading a group and climbing to the top of an organization are two different types of goals requiring two different behavior sets. It's OK to put alpha climbers into a group leadership role if they can deliver. In fact, if climbers got tested on their delivery capabilities at junior levels, a lot of them might wash out before getting high enough into the organization to derail a good culture.

In a luck-optimizing culture, leadership is allowed to spring up when and where it is needed. Titles and offices are not required for a leader to operate. However, if a junior leader is good, and is consistently able to get business results, a real title or position in the company might be a good idea.

FINAL THOUGHTS ON THE LUCK-OPTIMIZING CORPORATE CULTURE

In a team of well-selected players, the same factors that create fault tolerance also create luck optimization. Even when players are suboptimal performers, a group is generally more fault tolerant than an individual because if the individual can't perform the required task, that's it; nothing gets done. However, even in a poorly performing team, if a given person can't do the task, there are other people who probably can make sure that task gets done. That's the most basic fault-tolerant advantage that groups have over individuals.

But there is a much greater upside in groups, especially if the members are carefully selected. On the luck-optimizing side, a strong team will cover the basic practices described throughout this book. Not everyone is strong on all characteristics, but most people are really strong on some. Therefore, as part of a team each person becomes a better performer because somewhere in the team the strength can be found to handle any practice that a good corporate culture should exhibit. The addition of strong team players who understand luck optimization and fault tolerance helps us make up for our weaknesses. Attempts at corporate-level luck optimization and fault tolerance will work best with great players around us expanding the power of these ideas throughout the organization.

INDEX